IRISH GARDENS

From the Editors of

Country Living

GARDENER

Hearst Books, New York

IRISH GARDENS

Olda FitzGerald

Photography by Stephen Robson

Dedication
This book is for Desmond

Hearst Books

It is the policy of William Morrow and Company, Inc., and its imprints and affiliates, recognizing the importance of preserving what has been written, to print the books we publish on acid-free paper, and we exert our best efforts to that end.

Library of Congress Cataloging-in-Publication Data available upon request.

Text copyright © Olda FitzGerald 1999
Design and layout copyright ©
Conran Octopus 1999

Photography © Stephen Robson 1999
Garden Plans © William Pounds 1999
Map of Ireland © Lesley Craig 1999

The right of Olda FitzGerald to be identified as the Author of this Work has been asserted by her in accordance with the Copyright, Designs and Patents Act 1988. Color origination by Sang Choy International, Singapore. Printed in China.

ISBN 0-688-16885-X

Commissioning Editor Stuart Cooper
Editor Helen Woodhall
Editorial Assistant Alexandra Kent
Copy Editor Annie Reid
Index Helen Snaith

Art Editor Isabel de Cordova/Pep Sala
Picture Research Jessica Walton
Illustrator William Pounds
Production Oliver Jeffreys

First Edition
1 2 3 4 5 6 7 8 9 10

www.williammorrow.com
ci-gardener.com

List of Irish Gardens

1. Altamont
2. Annes Grove
3. Ardcarraig
4. Ballinlough Castle
5. Ballymaloe Cookery School Gardens
6. Birr Castle
7. Butterstream
8. Creagh
9. Derreen
10. The Dillon Garden
11. Glenveagh Castle
12. Glin Castle
13. Ilnacullin
14. Kilfane Glen and Waterfall
15. Killruddery
16. Mount Stewart
17. Mount Usher
18. National Botanic Gardens, Glasnevin
19. Rowallane
20. Woodfield

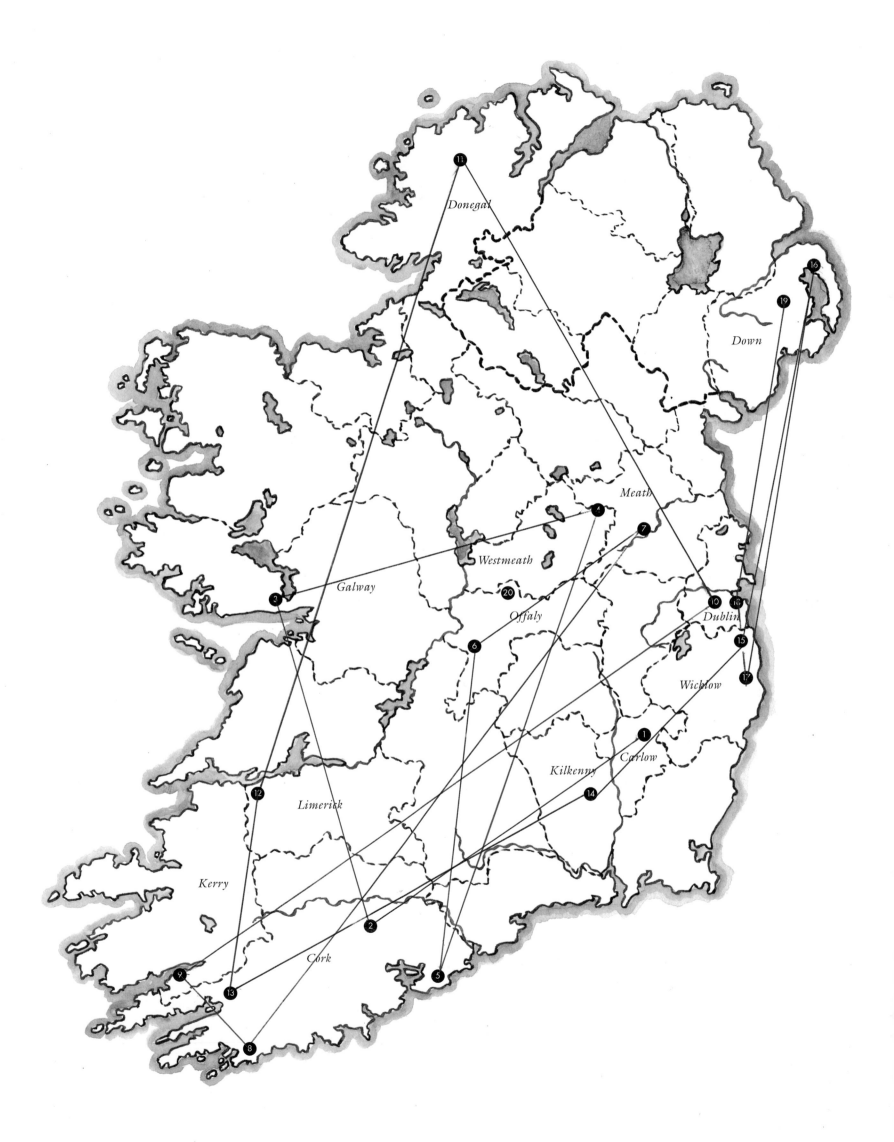

CONTENTS

Introduction 8

Altamont   *County Carlow*   22

Annes Grove   *County Cork*   32

Ardcarraig   *County Galway*   42

Ballinlough Castle   *County Westmeath*   52

Ballymaloe Cookery School Gardens   *County Cork*   60

Birr Castle   *County Offaly*   70

Butterstream   *County Meath*   82

Creagh   *County Cork*   94

Derreen   *County Kerry*   104

The Dillon Garden   *Ranelagh, Dublin*   114

Glenveagh Castle   *County Donegal*   124

Glin Castle   *County Limerick*   134

Ilnacullin   *County Cork*   144

Kilfane Glen and Waterfall   *County Kilkenny*   154

Killruddery   *County Wicklow*   162

Mount Stewart   *County Down*   174

Mount Usher   *County Wicklow*   184

National Botanic Gardens, Glasnevin   *Dublin*   194

Rowallane   *County Down*   204

Woodfield   *County Offaly*   212

Visitor's Guide   220

Index   222

Acknowledgments   224

INTRODUCTION

I hope that opening this book will be like opening the lid of a box filled with such delights that no one who looks inside will be able to resist exploring the glories of these Irish gardens. Not only are they all places of great beauty, but they also show the amazingly colorful and absorbing history of Irish plants and gardens. In each chapter I have explored a single garden, and have attempted to reveal its deeper secrets. It has been a journey through time and space – each garden represents at least a lifetime's work, and wise and knowledgeable gardeners have helped me at every turn to listen to the many voices of the past.

It has been an exciting – sometimes painful – challenge to select only 20 out of the many gardens that are open to the public. I have selected gardens that are not just personal favorites, but ones whose designs clearly illustrate a particular period of garden history, and whose plantings demonstrate an almost obsessional love of plants and the Irish landscape.

Previous page, main picture: The rushing water of the River Camcor in front of Birr Castle seen through cherry blossom on leafless branches in early spring.

Previous page, detail: The deep blue of massed banks of this hollyhock in the walled garden at Glin Castle in June.

Many of the gardens featured have benefited from the extraordinary number of exotic plants that became available on the return of the great plant-hunters in the late nineteenth and early twentieth centuries, and by the theories of naturalistic gardening propounded by the Irishman William Robinson. Others have combined the formal with the informal, and others have concentrated on the discovery and preservation of gardens that had either been hidden for many years or were about to disappear into the jungle. Every garden featured has a story to tell, and the gardeners who created or resurrected them are the heroes and heroines of these stories. All the gardeners I met or researched in the writing of this book combine an iron determination with a wild but discriminating enthusiasm.

Much has been lost in the turbulent passage of time, but, in remarkable instances of tenacity, the gardens of Killruddery, Birr Castle, Derreen,

Altamont, Annes Grove, Glin Castle, Ballinlough Castle, and Woodfield have been saved and, in some cases, recreated by the families who have always owned them. The National Botanic Gardens at Glasnevin and the gardens of Glenveagh Castle and Ilnacullin have been taken into the fostering care of Dúchas, the Heritage Service of the Department of Arts, Heritage, Gaeltacht and the Islands, while those at Mount Stewart and Rowallane are in the dependable hands of the National Trust. Ardcarraig, Butterstream, and The Dillon Garden are gardens made by the living owners, while Mount Usher, Creagh, Ballymaloe Cookery School and Kilfane are gardens of the past, cared for by the people who have imaginatively resuscitated them.

Gardening in Ireland has a long and checkered history. In the Iron Age, the Celts made a list in severe hierarchical fashion of the trees and shrubs they considered to be the chieftains, commoners, and peasants, according to

their usefulness and strength, from the great oak down to the completely disregarded wild rose. Standing in my own garden at Glin Castle, I take great comfort in the fact that, looking around, I can see each tree on the early Celtic list flourishing happily, either within the trimmer boundaries of cultivation or growing wild in hedge and woodland, and I feel a curiously visceral link with those first stubborn cultivators of this rich but sodden soil.

The Romans called Ireland Hibernia (Winter), but never crossed the Irish Sea to find out if this assumption was true. It is safe to assume, therefore, that gardening began to filter through from Europe with the advent of Christianity and the arrival of the Roman-educated followers of St. Patrick. The Venerable Bede (673–735AD) wrote: "Ireland is far more favored than Britain by latitude and by its mild and healthy climate … no need to store hay in summer … snow rarely lies more than three days … nor reptiles, no snake can exist here … milk and honey … no lack of vines." The effect of the warm waters of the Gulf Stream washing the coasts of the island was clearly making itself felt then as now. The warm southwest winds maintain the mild, damp climate, which means that plants and trees from all over the world do spectacularly well.

Early monastic settlements in the seventh and eighth centuries were surrounded by enclosures, within which were grown peas, beans, and leeks, as well as staple agricultural crops of wheat, oats, and barley. There were apple trees and beehives and "proper, rich, edible nuts," according to Maedoc of Ferns. Maolan, an early Irish lyricist, sings of the nuts and berries and apple trees near his hut and of the honeysuckle and strawberries. In Clonmacnoise, County Offaly, a gardener was surnamed Fionnscolaigh because of "the abundance of white flowers in his tyme."

The early missionary monks must have brought seeds and plants with them after returning from their studies in the great schools of learning in continental Europe. Woad, for example, was used to produce the blue dye for the scribes to use in their meticulously illuminated manuscripts of the Holy Scriptures. When looking at the ruins of the great monasteries and abbeys, it is easy to imagine their sheltered fruitful gardens and self-sufficient communities. Our Lady of the Fertile Rocks at Corcomroe in the Burren is a Cistercian abbey, where the beautiful limestone capitals of the columns are carved, each with a different flower. These, the earliest botanical carvings in Western Europe, date from 1205. The Irish medieval complex would have included different enclosures for vegetables, flowers, and herbs. In addition to beehives, fishponds, a dovecote, and an orchard of apples and pears, the abbots' and scribes' gardens would have been surrounded, if possible, by a deer park. Hunting wild deer was a favorite sport, and the medieval Irish deer park was the precursor of the eighteenth-century Irish landscape park, such as Ballyfin, County Laois.

After the Norman Conquest, the Norman families built their tower houses and settled down, becoming, as the saying goes, "more Irish than the Irish themselves," their military experience reflected in the efficient organization of their estates. Fishponds and warrens teemed with life, deer ran in the oak-

Opposite: The turrets and battlements of Lismore Castle seen through the boughs of a fruitful apple tree in one of the oldest gardens in the country.

Below: A walk of ancient yews at Lismore Castle.

fenced park, and there were walled falconries. In 1238, a gardener at Old Ross in County Wexford was paid for bedding out herbs and leeks, and one has the impression of a complex of enclosed gardens surrounding the great central court of the manor.

The first written work on gardening in the English language by "Master Jon Gardener" was copied by a fourteenth-century scribe in County Kildare. It mentions lilies, roses, lavender, camomile, and rosemary, and "all the herbs of Ireland." Although gardening was well established by the mid-sixteenth century, it took a while for interest in native plants to spread. In the 1580s, Lord Leicester and Mr. Secretary Walsingham began to grow saplings of the strawberry tree (*Arbutus unedo*), a newly discovered rarity, sent to them from Killarney. Legend has it that Sir Walter Raleigh introduced the potato into Ireland. He is also said to have brought sweetly scented wallflowers from the Azores and the tobacco plant from America, and grown them all in the walled garden at his Elizabethan house, Myrtlegrove in Youghal, County Cork (which still exists). The Great Earl of Cork, ancestor of the present owner, the Duke of Devonshire, bought Lismore Castle from Sir Walter in 1626, and created what is now one of the oldest gardens in the country.

At the end of the seventeenth century, exotic trees were already being planted in the great demesnes, and the first primitive greenhouses were built. New varieties of shrubs were imported, including the variegated ones which were gilt box and gilt holly. In 1692, Sir Arthur Rawdon of Moira in the north of Ireland filled his conservatory with 1,000 tropical plants, which he had sent his gardener to search for and bring back from Jamaica. A physic garden had been started on the campus of the University of Dublin, and by the 1720s it contained plants from distant places, including Africa.

The word "demesne" is a uniquely Irish term which has survived from medieval times. It was used to describe the lands surrounding a manor that were kept by a lord for his use, so that the demesne remained a distinct entity until the early twentieth century, when the Windham Land Acts finally dismantled the Irish estate system. The demesnes of Ireland occupy a central place in the evolution of the landscape, comprising areas of architectural, archeological, and botanical importance. Their distinctive layouts, which incorporate farmland, gardens, woods, and buildings, still form a dominant manmade component of the landscape.

After King Charles II came to the throne in 1660, the size of formal garden layouts increased to provide suitable settings for the mansions being built in Ireland at the time. Influences flooded in from Europe via Holland and France, and in the 1690s Renaissance ideas caught the imagination of the great landowners. Contemporary paintings show great houses surrounded by a dense mesh of radiating and converging avenues planted across the surrounding parkland. It was only from an elevated perspective that a true idea could be given of the unity of the overall design, and thereby the extent of the wealth and control of the owner through his "geometry of power." In these pictures, it is enthralling to see the details of canals with swans and fountains, mounts overlooking terraces, and tiny figures walking in the groves.

Gardening style is also influenced by changing fashions as much as time, and when Queen Anne removed the elaborate parterres from the garden of Hampton Court in 1703, at once a similar fate befell the flowers and boxwood hedging in front of Irish houses. Embroidered patterns of boxwood, colored gravel, and flowers were wiped away in favor of a simpler parterre of panels and slopes of mown grass outlined by gravel. Ironically, at the moment when horticulture was reaching a new height of interest, flowers were banished to walled gardens. There were flower clubs, however, whose members met in taverns once a month in Dublin, competing for prizes offered for the best auriculas and polyanthus raised from seed.

The fashion for formal gardens spread all across the country. Typically, owners would look across their boxwood knot gardens, and through the wrought iron gates in the wall and down along a distant tree-lined vista to a canal and circular pond. Everyone who was anyone had a canal à la Versailles. The earliest and most complete surviving garden of this date is at Killruddery. In the north of Ireland, Antrim Castle, home of Lord Massareene, is nearly as old. Mrs. Delany was to note faintly disparagingly in 1758: "Lady Massareene

Opposite top: Ballyfin, Co. Laios by Thomas Roberts, engraved by Thomas Milton in his Views from the Different Seats...in Ireland *1783–1793.*

Opposite bottom: Detail of the panoramic view of Stradbally Hall, Co.Laios. *(Private Collection) c.1740.*

Above: This plate from Thomas Wrighte's Grotesque Architecture *published in 1767 was the inspiration for the rustic arch at Belvedere, Co. Westmeath.*

Above: The sun shining on the toy fort called "Gibraltar" in the middle of the lake at Larchill, Co. Kildare.

lives there in a very old house, the garden reckoned a fine one 40 years ago, high hedges and long narrow walks." At Pakenham Hall, now Tullynally Castle, home of the Pakenham family, the outlines of the lost formal layout of avenues and canals can just be seen stretching away from the house and are visible in very dry summers through the grass of the front field.

Gradually, the landed estates were established, and the face of the country-side was transformed by the agricultural improvements of drainage, enclosure, roadmaking, and fertilization. Fashions changed again, and all the geometric designs were swept away, walls and hedges were broken down to let in the countryside – nature and the serpentine line were all the rage. The walled fruit, vegetable, and flower garden, now with heated greenhouses, was relocated near the stables and out of sight of the house, so as not to disturb the pastoral peace or bring even a hint of economic reality into the picture.

Mrs. Pendarves, a widow who was later to become the wife of Dean Patrick Delany, was a seminal figure in Irish gardening, dancing through the pages of history both literally and metaphorically. As a young widow, in the 1730s she visited Ireland for the first time, staying up dancing every night –

sometimes until two in the morning. Her letters record whom she met, where she went, and details of the houses she stayed in and the gardens she visited. She gardened, sketched, made grottoes and shell houses, painted flowers and plants, sewed and embroidered, and traveled all over the countryside. She returned to Ireland in the 1750s to marry the Dean, and became the mistress of Delville, near Glasnevin. Dean Delany and Jonathan Swift (author of *Gulliver's Travels* and Dean of St. Patrick's Cathedral in Dublin) were great friends, with a common interest in landscape gardening. They had been to stay with the poet Alexander Pope, whose garden at Twickenham was planted in the new informal manner. They listened to his ideas, in which he urged a return "to the amiable simplicity of nature." "Let Nature never be forgot ..." he wrote, "consult the Genius of the Place in all." And he scorned "the ill taste of those who are so fond of Evergreens (Particularly Yews which are the most tonsile) as to destroy the nobler Forest trees, to make way for such little ornaments as Pyramids of dark green continually repeated, not unlike a Funeral procession." Both Deans on their return beautified their gardens in the new romantic manner, and were generous with advice to their friends.

Shortly before her marriage to the Dean, Mrs. Delany had visited Richard Wesley, the first Lord Mornington and grandfather of the first Duke of Wellington, who had been making many improvements to his demesne at Dangan, County Meath. She was enchanted by his irregularly shaped lake of 26 acres with a splendidly detailed miniature fort and several ships, one a complete man-of-war. She records: "The ground as far as you can see every way is waving in hills and dales, and every remarkable point has either a tuft of trees, a statue, a seat, and an obelisk or a pillar." Today the neighboring *ferme ornée* of Larchill, which must have been copied from Dangan, is being restored, complete with its original fort in the center of a lake, several eye-catchers including a fox's set made into a temple for the eighteenth-century eccentric owner to return to in the afterlife, rare breeds of pigs and goats, and a walled garden with statues, containing the original shell-decorated tower.

At Belvedere in County Westmeath, the garden follies and famous "Jealous Wall" are being mended, and the planting of the terraces and perennial beds revived. The "Jealous Wall" is a teetering stone profile of what appears to be a ruined castle with gothic windows and jagged outline, but is in fact a brilliant pastiche, just one wall thick, built by "wicked" Lord Belvedere, who imagined an affair between his wife and his brother who lived at Rochfort next door.

It is important to remember that gardens and parks in the eighteenth century were real-life versions of a pictorial ideal. For instance, the fashionable serpentine sheets of water at Carton, County Kildare (as painted by Thomas Roberts), were modeled on the peaceful landscape of a pastoral arcadian painting by Claude Lorrain. And the Dargle Valley in County Wicklow shown in an engraving by the Irish landscape painter George Barret is a version of what they had seen in the pictures of Salvatore Rosa. These two painters had become the two great inspirers of the natural garden. Gentlemen who had been on the obligatory "Grand Tour" in Europe and were inspired by the

Top: The Sheet of Water *at Carton, Co. Kildare, by Thomas Roberts c.1770. (Private collection)*

Above: The Dargle Valley, *an engraving by Georger Barret c.1755.*

Top: The cottage ornée *at Woodstock,
Co. Kilkenny, by Maria Spillsbury Taylor.
(National Gallery of Ireland)*

*Above: The thatched arbor at Glengariff
Castle, Co. Cork, c.1820. Artist unknown.
(Private collection)*

Italian countryside returned home with pictures in their baggage so they could use them as blueprints for their gardens. The setting of the Mussenden Temple, erected by Lord Bristol in his demesne at Downhill, County Londonderry (where there is now also a charming garden), is closely modeled on the painting by Claude Lorrain known as "Parnassus." In both the painting and the garden, a domed and circular temple is perched on the edge of a steep cliff at the bottom of which stretches an endless sea. Irish followers of Launcelot "Capability" Brown laid out belts of trees around the outer perimeter as well as sweeping lawns, hidden ditches, clumps and groves of trees, and lakes, with driveways meandering through parks. Everything was planned to give different views of the house, with huge feats of engineering involved in creating these "natural" landscapes. Parks were normally enclosed within walls, not just to keep people out, but also to provide employment in times of hardship – garden activity in the eighteenth and nineteenth centuries often accompanied periods of famine.

In the nineteenth century, formality returned once again to Irish gardening. The century was dominated by horticultural advances and by wooden packing cases filled with plants that arrived from the Argentine, California, Mexico, the Himalayas, China, and Australasia. The new Botanic Gardens in Belfast, Cork, and Dublin propagated the plants and then shared them with avid gardeners around the country. Lilies, orchids, rhododendrons, and cacti were among the spectacular plants first introduced through Ireland to gardens all over the world.

One of the great features of Victorian gardens was their dazzlingly beautiful and intricate heated greenhouses. Many of them were constructed by Richard Turner of the Hammersmith Iron Foundry, Dublin, including those in the Botanic Gardens at Kew, Belfast, and Glasnevin, Dublin. It is still possible to find these narrow-paned, curvilinear soaring beauties hanging by a thread, like the magnificent one joined onto the house at Ballyfin, in County Laois, and the one in the walled garden miles from the house at Clonyn Castle, outside Mullingar, County Westmeath, or at Marlfield in County Tipperary. To see an enormous 1890s range of glasshouses, study old photographs of Kylemore Castle in County Galway, which was designed by J.F.Fuller for the Manchester industrialist Mitchell Henry. The garden is being restored, and it is hoped that the great greenhouses will rise again.

The Great Gardens of Ireland Restoration Programme, funded by the European Regional Development Fund, in which grants are given on a matched basis with the owners in return for the gardens being open to the public, has undertaken the restoration of many of these Victorian and Edwardian gardens as well as earlier ones. Among them are the nineteenth-century gardens laid out by C.R.Cockerell at Loughcrew in County Westmeath in the middle of a wild and romantic demesne near the burial cairns of pre-Celtic chiefs. The gardens at Bantry House overlooking Bantry Bay in County Cork and the extraordinary demesne and ruined garden at Woodstock, County Kilkenny, with a freestanding circular Turner

conservatory, avenue of monkey puzzles, tepidarium, parterre, and *cottage
ornée* on a wooded precipice not far from the one at Kilfane, are two more of
the gardens being restored in this project.

The gardens at Tullynally Castle, County Westmeath, are open to the
public; they include a grotto, walled garden, Victorian summerhouse, pond
with "weeping-pillar" fountain, and lake with black swans. There are stands of
magnificent trees and a woodland walk planted with groups of unusual shrubs
from China collected and grown from seed by the present owner, Thomas
Pakenham, which surround an enamel-red Chinese pavilion. Many of the
formal gardens and vistas laid out by Lady Ardilaun at Ashford Castle, Cong,
County Galway, still exist, with the spray from the great jet of water blowing
in the wind as it falls into the huge stone circular pond on the lake side of the
famous castle hotel. Perhaps the only Victorian garden with thousands of
bedding plants still maintained and changed twice annually is at Powerscourt,
County Wicklow. Here the seventh Viscount Powerscourt plundered the
gardens of Italy, France, and Austria for inspiration and created a dramatic
amphitheater, with large round pond and central fountain reached by flights
of steps and descending terraces with statues, urns, and parterres, using the
wooded valley and Sugarloaf Mountain as a backdrop.

*Above: Original watercolor by George Miller,
which was the source for the reconstruction
of the* cottage ornée *at Kilfane, Co. Kilkenny.
(Royal Society of Antiquaries of Ireland)*

Above: A view, through the wrought-iron gate, of a pond and fountain ringed by metal tortoises, inside the walled enclosure designed by Sir Edwin Lutyens at Heywood, Co. Laios.

By the beginning of the twentieth century, the Victorian straitjacket that had held the natural shapes of plants and trees in check for so long was loosened by a concerted barrage of writing from the irrepressible William Robinson. His book *The Wild Garden* (1870) suggested that plants should be allowed to grow in a garden as if they were in the wild, a revolutionary idea in an epoch that had favored the planting of forced hothouse annuals in geometric patterns. Robinson had grown up in Ireland and had gained some of his inspiration from the wilder gardens of his native land. He believed that shrubs and plants should be allowed to grow to their full size, and that native plants should be allowed to mix with the ever-increasing riot of exotic species that were being sent back to Ireland and England by the great plant-hunters. He thought that if they were all planted together as if they had happened naturally, it would give the impression of a Garden of Eden, which he believed suited the flowing landscape of Ireland. He popularized the use of hardy perennials in garden design and encouraged old-fashioned garden flowers like hollyhocks, sunflowers, lilies, and roses.

On the heels of the discoveries of the Irish customs officer and plant collector Dr. Augustine Henry, and with the help of Sir Frederick Moore, the director of the Botanic Gardens at Glasnevin, a flood of exhilarating hardy species began to reach Ireland from China and the remote mountains of Tibet and Burma. They flourished in the Irish climate, and nurseries propagated and sold them. The Daisy Hill Nursery at Newry, the Slieve Donard Nursery at Newcastle, and Watson's Nursery in Dublin set standards of excellence, while the nursery at Lissadell, in County Sligo, stocked an impressive collection of alpines, with the result that alpine gardening flourished in different rock gardens all over the country. Colonel Hill Walker even started a Japanese garden in Tully, County Kildare, which still exists today.

Perhaps one of the most fruitful combinations of talents in the history of gardening was that of the architect Sir Edwin Lutyens and the gardener Miss Gertrude Jekyll. The gardens at Heywood in County Laois are a splendid example of their collaboration, and even though the house has gone, the eighteenth-century buildings and waterworks in the picturesque valley are being restored, and the great stone drum, pergola, and terraces, with fountain and *oeil de boeuf* windows built by Lutyens looking out over the landscape, remain unforgettable. It is to be hoped that the new planting plans drawn up by Graham Stuart Thomas in the style of Gertrude Jekyll, with carefully annotated border plans as a guide, will soon be restored.

Lord Talbot de Malahide, who died in 1976, was arguably the most knowledgeable Irish gardener of his time. He built an extraordinary collection at Malahide Castle, specializing in plants from Australasia and South America. The gardens, looked after today by Fingal County Council, still contain many of his discoveries. The Edwardian perennial beds at Killmurry in County Kilkenny have been recorded for posterity by Mildred Anne Butler, whose paintings recreate the atmosphere of those forgotten Irish walled gardens in the sunny afternoons before World War I. That world of privileged security has vanished, and it is only now that garden archeologists are beginning to take seriously what it contained.

So many old Irish plants have disappeared that it is important that the gardeners of today be encouraged to grow and propagate Irish varieties. Such a fragile part of Ireland's heritage must not be lost, or the memories forgotten of those who were born or worked in Ireland and whose gardens may have been swept away but whose names live on in the plants they discovered and saved. The interest in gardens today has broken through all boundaries, social, political, and religious. Fascinating new gardens are being made all over the country. The number of garden centers is burgeoning, and there are magazines and television programs, and an excitement about visiting gardens, that has never been there before. Garden and landscape design are once more career options, and the history of gardening is taught at universities, while the National Botanic Gardens at Glasnevin give student botanists and gardeners excellent training. I raise my glass to the ladies and gentlemen, especially expert plantsmen and plantswomen like Betty Farquhar, David Shackleton, Lady Moore, and Lord Talbot de Malahide, without whom this revolution would not have been possible, and who have kept the threads of Irish gardening knowledge alive to hand on to the next generation.

Below: The restored vegetable and herb garden at Hilton Park, Co. Monaghan, with the house in the background in which lives Lucy Madden, one of the best cooks in Ireland. She and her husband Johnny grow their own produce to cook and serve to the visitors who stay overnight.

ALTAMONT
COUNTY CARLOW

Altamont is situated in a remote place, hidden within the many winding lanes of County Carlow. After a sharp bend, you are confronted by a classical stone gateway of rusticated pillars topped with large stone balls supported by thin, curving stone necks, with two smaller gates on either side for pedestrians. On the other side of the gates a golden beech avenue tempts you in. Cows graze in the field beyond, and at the end of the day, rooks can be seen flying through the trees before going to roost. A collection of rare young mountain ash trees is planted up each side of the avenue in the protective shade of ancient beech trees.

Altamont became a legend in the lifetime of Mrs. Corona North, who owned the estate until her death in 1999, and is the result of her and her father's continuous work and attention. Often, her elegant wolfhound could be seen sitting languidly on the front steps of the old house, as silkies and bantams stalked the gravel driveway.

Previous page, main picture: The elegant trunks of the beech trees in the Nun's Walk wet with rain in the fall.

Previous page, detail: Celtic motif based on pre-historic carvings on the back of a seat which stands at the New Bridge.

Above: Springtime is magnolia time at Altamont.

Opposite above: In springtime the 100 steps lead through clumps of naturalized old-fashioned daffodils.

Opposite below: This wild boulder-strewn stream bed has the feel of an ice age about it.

Indeed, for many generations of the North family there has been a close bond with the countryside of County Carlow. Mrs. North was one of the last members of a dynasty who came to Ireland in the early 1600s, married into a local Quaker family, and later built the nearby house of Ballydarton. They were all masters of foxhounds, not only in Carlow but also in the Cotswolds and in Australia, and began by starting the nearby Tullow Hunt in 1808. When Robert Gray Watson (1821–1906), then Master of the Carlow Hunt, was told by a lawyer that he was about to inherit Rockingham Castle in England, he replied: "What would I be doing with a castle in England when I have Ballydarton, and the best pack of hounds in Ireland?" In 1923, Mrs. North's parents, Isobel and Fielding Lecky-Watson, rented and then bought Altamont.

Fielding Lecky-Watson was a noted plantsman, a sponsor of botanical expeditions, and a rhododendron fanatic. Therefore, when Mrs. North was born, she was named for his favorite rhododendron, 'Corona.' Over his lifetime he bought thousands of rhododendrons; some he grew in his greenhouse from seed, and others he collected from abroad. Sadly, in the early 1970s, many were killed during a sharp frost, having split their bark, being vulnerable due to a dry summer followed by a long, mild, and rainy fall. The remaining rhododendrons are now back in force, due to Mrs. North's diligent replanting.

The earliest parts of the garden date back to the eighteenth century. However, most of the structure that we see today dates from the 1850s, when the Borror family bought the demesne on the banks of the River Slaney. Thanks to the mass employment project in the post-Famine era, they were able to employ 100 men with horses and carts to dig out the 2½-acre lake that became the central focus of the garden. On returning from England, where she worked in the Forces during World War I, Mrs. North found that the garden had become so overgrown that no one had been able to get around the lake for seven years. It took several years of determined hard work to clear the lake of weeds, and move and save the rhododendrons around it. From spring to fall she toiled away in a flat-bottomed barge, moving and saving the rhododendrons, with the help of just one old man.

Mrs. North was always an enthusiastic planter of trees – she often used to travel abroad with the International Dendrology Society – and they are one of the glories of the demesne. When her father died in 1943, she returned to Altamont for good with her new husband and moved into the Keeper's Cottage. Here she made a charming garden and started the Arboretum with the seeds she had collected on a trip to South America. When she had begun planting trees in her twenties, her enthusiasm had been considered eccentric, but Lady Moore – the wife of Sir Frederick Moore, director of the National Botanic Gardens, and a noted plantswoman herself – had been delighted to discover the young Corona planting a noble fir (*Abies procera*) and had encouraged her interest. In the parkland of the demesne, the branches of the old chestnuts and limes reach down to the ground, and outside the bowfront of the house stands a pair of nineteenth-century weeping ashes.

On the death of her mother, aged 102, in 1986, Mrs. North moved back into the main house. The changes included making the drawing room into one room again and installing central heating. She also began to bake her own bread and make butter and yogurt from the creamy milk produced by her herd of Jersey cows. Mrs. North was a statuesque figure with turquoise-blue eyes. She had an enormous amount of energy and was immensely hospitable. In the summer it was rare to be able to reach her on the telephone until she stopped mowing late in the evening. The residential painting and gardening courses that she ran were extremely popular. She personally conducted tours of the gardens and would arrange delicious teas and cold lunches for visitors.

Against the west wing of the house, a fine *Rhododendron augustinii* (named after Augustine Henry, the famous Irish plant collector) planted by Fielding Lecky-Watson still flourishes; it is 35 feet high, its gnarled old stems still producing a prolific quantity of lavender-blue flowers each spring. Old peonies grow at its feet. In the shelter of the house, a *Magnolia* x *soulangeana* 'Alba' thrives near the *Eucryphia lucida*, as well as *Cornus kousa* hybrids such as 'Madame Butterfly,' 'Norman Hadden,' and 'China Girl,' with its green flowers and white bracts. Nearby, a *Clerodendrum trichotomum* with scented white flowers, which Mrs. North grew from a cutting given to her by the late Lord Rosse from Birr Castle in the 1950s, is still in its prime.

From the house, a long Broad Walk edged in boxwood and punctuated by Irish yews leads under an arch of golden yew to the glassy water of the lily-clotted lake. The circumferences of the 1850 Irish yews are now all restrained by corsets of string, and all of them are clipped into wonderful egg-shaped domes. The walk is bordered with old-fashioned roses such as 'Madame Hardy,' 'Madame Isaac Pereire,' and Mrs. North's favorite 'Céleste,' with its shell-pink flowers and blue-gray leaves. For spring color, the roses are underplanted with 40 different varieties of snowdrops, several groups of the luminously yellow *Narcissus* 'Hawera,' and different-colored tulips.

Below: Formal and informal elements are carefully blended beside the picturesque lake at Altamont.

The lake and its surroundings are reminiscent of a painted theater background by Oliver Messel, with the actors poised to come onstage. As you walk around the margin, two rusty swamp cypresses frame a view. Red maples glow in the wood among a forest of rhododendrons, with the original *Rhododendron* 'Corona' still there next to 'White Pearl'; in the evening a mist falls on the lake and swans dip their necks in the inky water.

Among the collection of low-growing conifers in the beds around the edges of the lake is *Pinus sylvestris* 'Hibernia,' which makes an interesting small gray-blue dome. Another noteworthy plant is the primrose 'Guinevere,'

*Top: The California tree poppy
(Romneya coulteri).*

*Above: Making Altamont more than a flower
garden, Corona North grew fruits of many
kinds, including the delicious sweet wineberry.*

which was bred in Ireland in the 1930s. It has bronze leaves and pink flowers with a lemon-colored eye and, because of its good constitution, it is still thriving many years after other primroses have disappeared.

The huge expanse of sloping lawn on the other side of the lake is framed by giant trees, such as a many-stemmed *Thuja plicata* on a carpet of *Anemone blanda* and *Puschkinia*, a Deodar cedar, and a fern-leaved beech. By the lake stands a tulip tree (*Liriodendron tulipifera*) and a *Davidia involucrata*, with pure-white handkerchiefs, among the first trees planted by Mrs. North. There are unexpected views everywhere. "I like making vistas all over the place leading from one picture to another," she explained, "but this sends people who like great panoramas completely mad." The three islands on the lake are thickly planted – pampas grass and New Zealand flax provide the architectural element among the waterside plantings of candelabra primulas, fair-maids-of-France (*Ranunculus aconitifolius*), lilies, hostas, foxgloves, and dicentra.

Setting off beyond the lake, past the Myshall Gate, through groups of birches, southern beech, and the scarlet Chilean fire-bush, you come to a Bog Garden almost swamped by the huge leaves of the giant Chilean rhubarb (*Gunnera manicata*). From here the stream flows through an Ice Age glen, where thousands of years ago great boulders came to rest. There is a gap in the trees, where the stream unexpectedly becomes a waterfall, crashing hundreds of feet down into the River Slaney. Suddenly you are out into the clearing with the great wide sweep of river, and wild, untouched woods on each side stretching ahead in an almost medieval landscape. Here, as elsewhere, Mrs. North has taken advantage of every inch of scenery, with each twist and turn used to advantage in a subtle and intoxicating combination of surprises. Walking along the riverbank, you come to a staircase of 100 steps built into the steep hill of woodland. After walking up the dark staircase, through tunnels cut in the laurel thickets on the hillside, it is a welcome contrast to be led onto a high, open clearing surrounded by the green fields of County Carlow filled with sheep. Looking back from the High Ridges Walk, you can see the dense, confining woods. Ahead of you in the distance are the Blackstairs Mountains, crowned by the gentle peak of Mount Leinster.

Many of the trees at Altamont have interesting and personal histories. On the way back to the lake, you pass a giant redwood, or Wellingtonia (*Sequoiadendron giganteum*), belatedly planted to commemorate the Duke of Wellington's victory at the Battle of Waterloo of 1815 – it used to be surrounded rather picturesquely and appositely by a crown of Portuguese laurel. A balsam poplar (*Populus balsamifera*), now 100 feet high, was brought back by Mrs North from Dame Flora MacLeod from the Scottish Isle of Skye, and the storm-battered but still lovely *Prunus* 'Ukon' with creamy green flowers was planted 50 years ago by Mrs. North's father. The nuns who lived at Altamont in the seventeenth century are commemorated in an avenue of towering beech trees called the Nuns' Walk, which runs along the whole of one side of the garden, carpeted in turn through the seasons with vinca, Lent lilies, and fall-flowering cyclamen. Walking under the thick canopy of trees,

you turn right past a clipped boxwood hedge and are suddenly confronted again by the pink house which is hung with creepers – and a pair of doves more often than not sitting on the roof. Here, in a side courtyard, a 150-year-old sweet-smelling climbing rose, 'Blush Noisette', supports the deep blue *Clematis* 'Lasurstern.'

To one side of the house is the Walled Garden, in which an ornamental herb and vegetable garden flourishes. In one of the two greenhouses, 'Black Hamburgh' vines have been producing small sweet grapes for 150 years. There are also displays of the many varieties of the shrubs and trees in the gardens, all of which are for sale alongside delicious cakes and restorative tea.

The word "magical" is often used to describe the atmosphere of this garden, although the endeavor that has gone into keeping it is purely human. If it had not been for the single-minded determination, skill, and energy of Corona North, it would not be what it is today. She formed the Altamont Garden Trust to preserve this uniquely beautiful Irish demesne with its many thousands of plants and abundance of wildlife, and to save it from the bulldozers that have been the fate of so many Irish gardens. Now, after her death, it will go to the care of Dúchas, the Heritage Service of the Department of Arts, Heritage, Gaeltacht and the Islands. My generation and that of my children owe her a tremendous debt of thanks.

Above: Orange pot marigolds, variegated nasturtiums, cabbages, and herbs, including purple sage and fennel, can provide just as colorful a garden as more exotic plants. Everything in the formal potager is edible, including the tall artichokes that have been allowed to blossom.

Plan of Altamont

1. Walled Garden
2. Potager & Herb Garden
3. Nun's Walk
4. Celtic Motif
5. New Bridge
6. Temple Folly
7. High Ridges Walk
8. River Slaney & 100 steps
9. Sunset Field
10. Ice Age Glen
11. Boulder Strewn Stream
12. Bog Garden
13. New Arboretum
14. Lake
15. Iron Bridge
16. Broad Walk

ANNES GROVE
COUNTY CORK

The square eighteenth-century house of Annes Grove is all but buried by a lush growth of creeping vines. Wands of kiwi fruit cascade over the windows and at its back, the ground falls away in terraces to the river.

Annes Grove was brought to public attention in 1776 by Arthur Young in his *Tour of Ireland*. In fact, it was the only garden mentioned, and it was noted that the estate was rented at the time by the Aldworth family. "Mrs. Aldworth," writes Arthur Young approvingly, "has ornamented a beautiful glen, which winds behind the house, in a manner that does honour to her taste; she has traced her paths so as to command all the beauties of rock, wood and a sweet river which glides beneath both; it is a most agreeable scenery." The same could be said today, but the eighteenth-century vista must have shown the river against the bare gorge of the limestone cliffs, which are now covered with shrubs and trees – a patchwork of green until the fall months, when it changes to magnificent bronze and gold.

Inheriting a famous and beautiful garden created by your grandfather is a challenge, but, with the voices of his ancestors ringing in his ears, one that Patrick Annesley welcomed. In 1973 Patrick gave up his career as a publisher in London to return with his wife Jane to Annes Grove to look after the garden and to bring up their children in the family home.

The property had belonged to the Grove family since the seventeenth century. In 1764, Mary Grove, the heiress, married Francis, soon to be the first Earl Annesley, who built the house and later rented it to Mrs. Aldworth. The Annesleys were childless, so the estate passed to their nephew Arthur, who called himself Grove Annesley. Arthur's son Richard who "Victorianized" the Walled Garden in the 1860s, adding flowerbeds full of delphiniums and building a viewing mound. He packed the ribbon beds of boxwood with pocketbook flowers and primroses, and also planted the yew walk.

Richard Grove Annesley's son, also named Richard, inherited Annes Grove in 1907. He had a keen interest in gardening and had many connections in the Irish gardening community, including his cousin, Earl Annesley of Castlewellan, County Down (which is now the National Arboretum). Others were Hugh Armytage Moore of Rowallane, Gerard Leigh White of Bantry House, the Bryces of Illnacullin, and Sir Frederick and Lady Moore of the Botanic Gardens at Glasnevin. It is Richard who is said to have encouraged the trees and plants on the cliffs to grow by standing in front of the rock and firing laburnum and aubrieta seeds with his catapult into the cracks!

There was a 12-year hiatus at the beginning of the century. Richard served with the North Irish Horse in World War I and subsequent troubles in Ireland prevented him from concentrating on his gardening. Afterward, Richard returned to his garden with increased vigor. Before the war he had snapped up the opportunity to try to grow showy hybrid rhododendrons. Later, he subscribed to the first of a series of syndicates established by garden owners to sponsor the plant-hunting expeditions of Captain Frank Kingdon Ward in Burma and Tibet. Some of the hair-raising reports of these expeditions to the remote Himalayan valleys are still kept in the house at Annes Grove. Richard planted some of the rhododendron seeds brought back from these expeditions on one of the slopes at the back of the house. They took so well that they look today as if they were growing in the wild. Planted alongside were well-known woodland exotics of that period, such as the Chilean fire-bush (*Embothrium coccineum*) and Chile lantern bush (*Crinodendron hookerianum*) from South America, eucryphia, New Zealand daisy bushes (*Olearia*), and North American dogwoods. The Robinsonian influence is evident here in the large number of exotic species thriving alongside native flora, all growing together in glorious informality.

As you walk around the edge of the path from the house to the beginning of the shrubby walk that forms the backbone of these planted slopes, the scent of vanilla from the *Azara microphylla* 'Variegata' drifts through the air. This plant originated in the garden of one of the great Victorian names in Irish horticulture, W.E.Gumbleton, J.P., of Belgrove, near Cobh, County Cork.

Previous page, main picture: The rampant kiwi fruit that curtains the outside of Annes Grove is a relative newcomer from China, introduced hardly a century ago. The house, twice this age, commands a view over the glen and River Awbeg, around which a garden was created in the 1760s.

Previous page, detail: Fall-flowering cyclamen emerging from a carpet of cedar needles.

Opposite: Under the moss-covered trunk of a magnolia, there is a colorful array of naturalized spring flowers, including Spanish bluebells, simple yellow Welsh poppies, and a sprinkling of rose-pink tulips. This is gardening at its least stressful.

Below: Wild primroses provide a splash of colour under a beech tree in the spring.

Above: The graceful gray-green serrated foliage of Melianthus major, *a native of South Africa, is often seen in Irish gardens.*

Opposite: The hybrid Japanese anemone (Anemone x hybrida) *was raised at Chiswick, in London, in the middle of the nineteenth century. It is a vigorous perennial that flowers for a long period in late summer.*

The showy green leaves of a catalpa and the white blossoms of a self-seeded lacebark tree combine with the autumnal pink-tipped Persian ironwood tree and sharp spines of *Colletia hystrix* in a spectacular display. Light filters through the trees onto groups of dogwoods and the snowy-white flowers of *Cornus kousa* var. *chinensis.* The small glossy *Rhododendron* 'Blue Tit' leads to *R. falconeri,* with its creamy blossoms loosely packed like Christmas bells. Pink and white azaleas and the blue *Rhododendron augustinii* are next to the scarlet 'May Day', and *R. thomsonii* has red waxy flowers with yellow centers.

Walking toward the house from the Rhododendron Garden, you come across a rock face covered with hydrangeas, whose china-blue, pink, and bronze flowers tumble down to the river level. A *Magnolia macrophylla* has leaves 2 feet long, which some visitors mistake for the leaves of a banana tree. The sun falls through the branches of the sheltering pines onto the *Rhododendron sinogrande,* whose new growth resembles Romaine lettuce (because of the silvered undersides of the leaves). The sad-looking coffin tree, *Juniperus recurva* var. *coxii* 'Castlewellan,' presumably a present to Richard from his cousin, stands next to a slender peeling eucalyptus and the *Rhododendron* 'Lady Chamberlain', with her very orange trumpet. A line of 300-year-old tangled linden trees skirts the outside of the Walled Garden on the north side; this cuts the path and continues into the field that defined the boundary of the eighteenth-century garden. The family silver is said to be buried beneath one of the trees, though treasure-seekers may be deterred by the ghost of a lady holding a flaming sword; she's believed to drive men mad.

Descending to the river via mossy stone steps, there seem to be at least 40 shades of green on the opposite bank. The river runs beneath groves of rustling bamboo and wild meadowsweet (*Filipendula ulmaria*). Swaths of color from the umbrella plant (*Darmera peltata*) and the autumn-pink leaves of the katsura tree (*Cercidiphyllum japonicum*) show up against the vast dark green leaves of the ubiquitous giant rhubarb (*Gunnera manicata*). A solitary Siberian crab apple stands next to the tallest gray poplar. Native rush and sedge, the flag iris, and butterbur (*Petasites*) form a background for the candlelike Himalayan primulas and the ivory and yellow cowls of the skunk cabbages (*Lysichiton*). Water gardens had captured the imagination of the late Victorians through the paintings of the Pre-Raphaelites, and Richard used a detachment of British soldiers stationed in the nearby town of Fermoy to dig out and clear the eighteenth-century artificial canal. He changed the geometry of the old garden, remaking many of the paths down to the river and clearing the whole bank so that he could plant exotic introductions from America, the high Alps, and the Himalayas, including Tibetan and Chinese poppies. He even contrived to make the river flow backward around a little island. Rustic bridges draped in wisteria criss-cross the swirling water, while in true Monet fashion colonies of water lilies spatter the calm backwaters and tributaries of the curving River Awbeg.

Making the Himalayan climb back up the winding steps and across the path that forms the spine of the garden, you come to the Walled Garden.

Left: Fall leaves soften the contours of moss-covered steps.

Right: A rustic wooden bridge spanning the River Awbeg is almost hidden by the enormous leaves of the giant Chilean rhubarb, which is so at home in Annes Grove.

Following the fashions of Edwardian England, Richard Grove Annesley turned it into outside "rooms" by dividing it into compartments with a series of beech and yew hedges. In one of its compartments, a curved pond is surrounded by hostas, ornamental grasses, rodgersias, and other waterside plants in a way that the current owner, Patrick, thinks was deliberately made to echo the planting by the river. A twisted birch resembling a weeping willow contributes to the Japanese feel of this part of the garden, which is attributed to Patrick's grandmother. Under a magnolia, Welsh poppies, purple tulips, Solomon's seal (*Polygonatum*), and wild garlic are all planted against the heavenly blue of alkanet (*Anchusa*), which spreads outward in a great cloud.

In another compartment, lush perennial beds are planted against the dark background of a yew hedge. On limestone flagstones from County Clare stands a sundial dated 1705. It is encased in an Arts and Crafts stone base, with the words "I only count the sunny hours" engraved on the top in Gaelic.

An avenue of dark yews leads away from the "rooms", forming a shady tunnel at the end of which you can see a greenhouse that has been painted white. Since the walled garden was originally an orchard, the walls facing west and south are lined with brick to retain the heat so appreciated by the fan-trained peach and nectarine trees. Next to the late beds of purple, mauve, and white Michaelmas daisies (asters) stands the Edwardian pergola, which is covered in honeysuckle, roses, vines, and a delicate butter-yellow clematis.

The formal rose beds are laid out in the shape of a Celtic cross, with a mixture of Old English and Hybrid Tea roses. Clipped hedges overrun by ribbons of the red creeper *Tropaeolum speciosum* form the boundary of this compartment, and roses tumble over the outer garden walls. Both the sumptuously glossy evergreen *Clematis armandii* and *Actinidia kolomikta* climb up the wall to meet the roses. A pretty ironwork gate leads onto a cobbled track and on through another gate until you reach the main garden. As you turn away from the garden, the house comes into view from around the corner of a mass of *Rhododendron ponticum*. A carpet of pink and white cyclamen under the cedar of Lebanon lies directly across from the front door.

The back of the house is draped with clematis, roses, jasmine, and white fuchsia. The dove house, too, is swathed with plants. One of the charming gate lodges that was on the brink of falling to pieces has been saved by Ireland's Landmark Trust. It has been beautifully restored and will sleep two people comfortably. Designed by Benjamin Woodward, it was the model for the gatehouse at University College, Cork. It has a spiral staircase and, in the writer Mary Leland's words, "just enough room to swing a kitten."

It is one of life's small miracles that this eighteenth-century Irish country estate, with all its interdependent parts, still exists in a completely unspoiled state, with the original family's descendants still in residence. Nowhere else can you find a garden of such sleepy charm and beauty, whose nostalgic atmosphere, far from being a mere recreation of past glories, is living proof of the dedication of its owners, both past and present.

Below: Cabbage palms from New Zealand, giant rhubarb from South America, bamboos from the Far East – all growing as William Robinson advocated. Annes Grove is an excellent example of a Robinsonian wild garden.

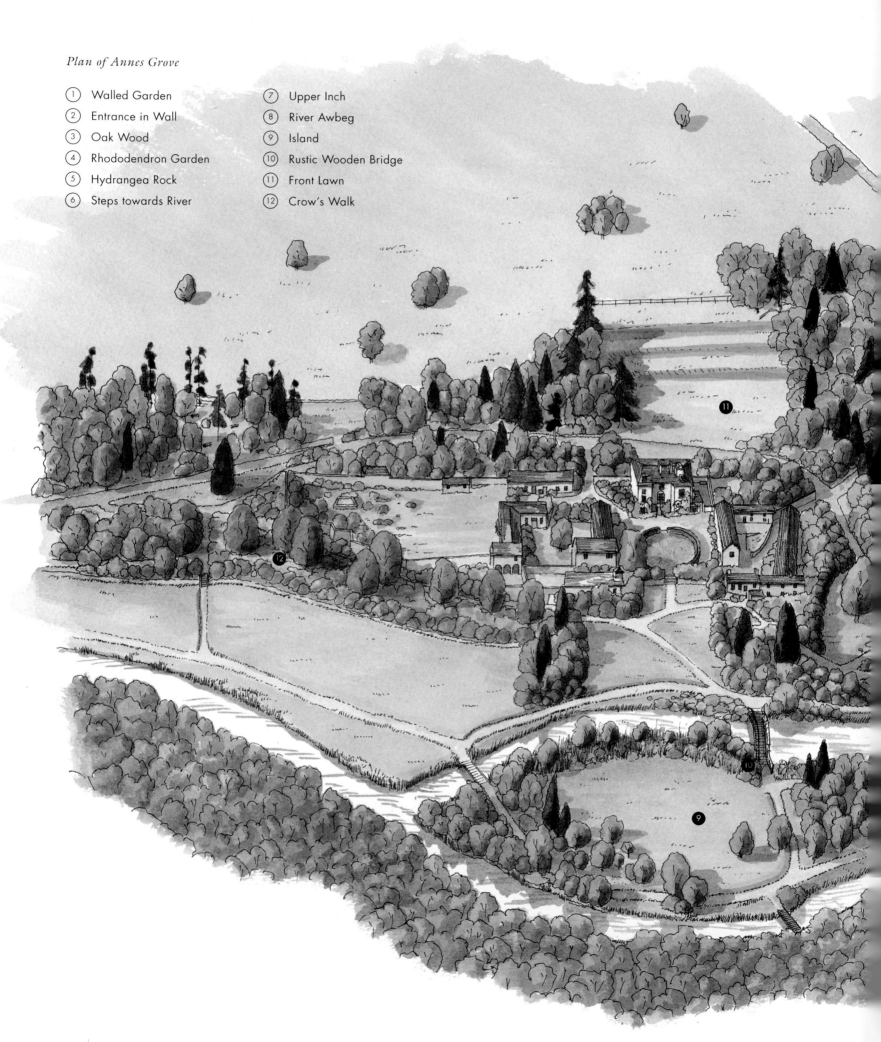

Plan of Annes Grove

1. Walled Garden
2. Entrance in Wall
3. Oak Wood
4. Rhododendron Garden
5. Hydrangea Rock
6. Steps towards River
7. Upper Inch
8. River Awbeg
9. Island
10. Rustic Wooden Bridge
11. Front Lawn
12. Crow's Walk

ARDCARRAIG

COUNTY GALWAY

Unless you had heard about it, you would never know this garden existed, hidden as it is in a lovely hazel wood. In fact, it is a series of small gardens, or enclosures, set in clearings on a windswept hillside, linked by rustic steps between the different levels.

In 1971, Lorna MacMahon and her late husband Harry bought the modern bungalow a short way outside Galway in the middle of what must have seemed unpromising terrain. North-facing, with thin acid soil and little shelter from the Atlantic winds, the growing season is short, and the rainfall averages 70 inches a year. This was Lorna's ninth garden, and it was a challenge she had never met before. All that existed were the boundary fences, the driveway, and the shell of a house. There was no soil: just rocks, gorse, heather, hazel scrub, and a howling southwesterly wind. However, to the north of the house Lorna had spotted a deep hollow in the front garden, in which she placed all her hope.

Previous page, main picture: Gardens in Ireland are fortunate to be able to combine in one place so many plants of different origins, colors, and textures, and then allow nature to do the rest. Lorna did plant the cowslips and the candelabra primulas, but now they seed themselves. The fountains of variegated New Zealand flax provide contrasting texture.

Previous page, detail: The orchid primula (Primula vialii) from Western China requires moist peaty soil. In the background are the variegated leaves of a New Zealand flax.

Before moving to Connemara, the MacMahons had lived for five years near the Botanic Garden in Edinburgh, Scotland. Here Lorna had fallen passionately in love with dwarf conifers, so one of the first things the couple did at Ardcarraig was to pour 34 loads of lime-rich topsoil into the front yard over the rocks to support a beech hedge and specimen trees. The dwarf conifers grew at such a rate that some have since had to be removed. The heathers and conifers, such as the golden weeping cedar (*Cedrus deodara* 'Gold Horizon') and the upright golden yew (*Taxus baccata* 'Fastigiata Aurea'), feel very much at home among the windswept Connemara hills. The weeping purple beech (*Fagus sylvatica* 'Purpurea Pendula'), on the other hand, is still only waist-high in spite of being 25 years old. Over time, this part of the garden has achieved a sense of balance and is now well planted,

with graceful taller shrubs, among which the red berries of the rowan tree and the lovely late-summer-flowering white blossoms of *Eucryphia lucida* provide a foil for the more solid shapes of the conifers. This is the quiet, respectable side of the garden. "Sweet disarray" follows in spring, when the serious-looking sharp-pinned dwarf conifers are enlivened by boisterous snowdrops and airy snowflakes (*Leucojum*), followed by crocuses and daffodils.

The first enclosure you encounter when walking around the house is a formal sunken garden, planted in memory of Lorna's fanatical gardening aunts. All their favorite flowers, from *Abutilon vitifolium* to *Callistemon sieberi*, are grown around the edge of the terrace; a large Cretan terracotta pot stands in the middle as a focal point. A pergola made out of railroad ties is covered by a lacy shawl of *Clematis tibetana* and *C. rehderiana*.

Above left: A healthy clump of various hostas demonstrate how the climate of County Galway is ideal for gardening.

Above: A snow-viewing lantern with a red maple and other plants all reflected in still water conjures up visions of Japan. The triangular rock representing Mount Fuji just happened to be in the right place.

Leaving this enclosure behind, you walk out into the magical shadows of a hazel wood. Mosses and lichens cover the bark of trees, and glacial boulders lie scattered about the wood, surrounded by a thick carpet of ivy and ferns. In spring, bluebells and wood anemones light up the forest floor. Hazel woods in Ireland are extremely precious. After the original oak woods were swept away by neolithic farmers, the countryside was dominated by hazel woods until they, in turn, were cut down during the final woodland clearance of Elizabethan times. Only a few isolated pockets remain, mainly in the west of Ireland, which is why Lorna MacMahon was absolutely determined to keep as much of the hazel wood as possible, confining her gardening to the areas that had thinned out naturally, leaving only scrub, willow, and bramble. Precedents for this style of garden are few: although Vita Sackville-West had already made a nuttery at Sissinghurst, in England, and nut tunnels made of hazel trees had been a formal feature of gardens for centuries, there were not many forerunners of a wild garden in a hazel wood for Lorna to copy.

The Mary O'Conor Garden is in the next clearing, created in memory of a great friend of Lorna's who, in the early 1970s, introduced a whole range of plants to County Galway via the County Galway Flower Club, including herbaceous perennials such as geraniums and unusual violas. Here you can see the blue waters of Lough Corrib over the tangle of clematis and the prolific white climbing roses 'Kiftsgate' and 'Rambling Rector' and the trees and shrubs. The branches of *Eucryphia glutinosa* and *Hoheria sextylosa* are heavy, borne down in summer full weight of their white flowers. From the Knight of Kerry's old garden in Valentia Island, County Kerry, comes the splendid *Myrtus luma* 'Glanleam Gold,' with its orange-scented blossoms and gilt-edged leaves, evoking images of Victorian brides with their bouquets of myrtle. Bright-green-leaved azaleas are tightly packed on the steep slope, while perennial cranesbills, such as *Geranium wallichianum* 'Buxton's Variety' flower in wild profusion.

The Primula Garden is packed, of course, with blue, pink, and white candelabra primulas, although there are also the limpid blue flowers of the Himalayan poppy (*Meconopsis grandis*). The high rainfall during the summer months means they flower really well in their rocky habitat, and they form large colonies in the black moorland soil in company with the purple and blue Siberian iris. Here there are also perennials, such as lily-of-the-valley, London pride, and the foam flower (*Tiarella cordifolia*). The parchment-white bark of the silver birch trees is a contrast to the cinnamon-colored trunks of the myrtles and the blood-red branches of the dogwoods. In late summer, dark blue hydrangeas and pink astilbes can just about be seen among the enormous spread of the giant Chilean rhubarb before it collapses.

When the MacMahons bought the next piece of land, it was a total jungle – so much so that they could hear a stream but could not see one anywhere. Lorna cleared away every bit of undergrowth, bush, and stone, so today the sparkling stream can be seen clearly as it winds its way through what is now

Top: The moist mild climate and shelter at Ardcarraig provide ideal conditions for growing ferns.

Above: There are about 1,200 flowering plants and ferns growing wild in Ireland that could be cultivated in gardens. Here a fern can be seen coming to life in the early part of the year, each frond unrolling like a coiled spring.

Opposite: Lorna has carefully retained the wild plants and ferns along the stream banks, but intermingled them with exotic poppies, primroses, and hostas. The yellow tutsan (Hypericun androsaemum) is a native shrub found in wild woods throughout Ireland.

Above: Early summer in one of the glades at Ardcarraig. Hostas, iris, and candelabra primulas weave a carpet of color with the darker green leaves of the giant Chilean rhubarb as a backdrop.

the Bog Garden. She had to bring all the soil and gravel in by wheelbarrow and dig out the pool by hand to prevent the stream from flooding. For the Bog Garden, Lorna chose ornamental trees especially for their bark or leaf color, such as snakebark maples, a *Gingko*, a *Metasequoia*, and different forms of cut-leaf beech. Hundreds of frogs leap through a clump of arctostaphylos. Lorna is trying to plant every space to avoid using weedkiller, and lithospermum (*Lithodora*) are allowed to seed and flower in these ideal boggy conditions. Lorna has circled all the surrounding areas with holly, hazel, and hawthorn to blend into the natural landscape, and she has planted lobelias and day lilies, which like their feet in water. All this endeavor is quite staggering, and Lorna is very philosophical about the future: "I have no illusions about finding anyone as cracked as I am to do what I do, but I have just had such fun and enjoyed it all so much." She sees herself carrying on for some time yet – and then, she shrugs, "nature will take the garden back."

In the two Japanese sections – one larger than the other – Lorna has combined Japanese inspiration with her own style of gardening. For instance, "they (the Japanese) would have clipped all the azaleas, but that would be completely against my nature," she explains. At every angle of every path, there is a new view. One particular view is of a Japanese hill and pool garden, complete with a genuine snow-viewing lantern (*Uki-mi-doro*), which was brought to Ireland by a former Thai ambassador. It is made of such solid granite and is so heavy that it would need a helicopter to move it out again. Hostas, Japanese maples, the golden form of the Japanese cedar *Cryptomeria japonica* 'Sekkan-sugi,' as well as *Sophora japonica* and several ravishing cherries, encircle the lantern. A large granite rock, conveniently already in place, represents Mount Fuji, and the pool is entirely surrounded by oriental plants and trees and striped Japanese ribbon grass.

In another clearing, named for her friends Mary Joe and Charlie Madden, who gave her so many unusual plants at the beginning of the garden's life, Lorna was able to nurture a number of marginally tender trees and shrubs in the sheltered and frostfree zone. Varieties of gum trees (*Eucalyptus*), pittosporum, and Australian bottlebrushes (*Callistemon*) all flourish against the remains of the stony walls of what Lorna discovered were two houses that had been abandoned during the Famine.

After Harry's death in 1996, Lorna was given so many plants by friends that she determined to make a garden dedicated to him. She prepared the ground, using a pickax to remove stones, and filled up the holes with new earth mixed with mushroom compost and horse manure. She planted the hillside mostly with azaleas for spring flowers and melaleuca for color in the summer months, with a number of low-growing Australian plants (dwarf callistemon and dwarf podocarps, for example) among the granite rocks and the sheltered pools. Soon there will be magnolias here, eucryphias, lomatias, dogwoods, stewartia, lily-of-the-valley bushes (*Pieris*), rowan trees, whitebeams (*Sorbus*), and southern beeches (*Nothogagus*), all rising above the wind line and making this the most beautiful section of all in the garden.

The Herb Garden is laid out as a knot garden in raised beds and containers on the old tennis court near the house. Many of the herbs grown are old-fashioned ones, mentioned in the Bible and Shakespeare's plays, such as sage and golden hops, interspersed with hollyhocks, alliums, and a little pansy called heartsease, whose other names are johnny-jump-up or love-in-idleness.

From just a small clearing back in 1971, Lorna has singlehandedly built the unique five-acre garden – seemingly against the odds. There had long been an attitude in the west of Ireland that it was wrong to spend money in planting decoratively because the area had been so deprived for so long. In addition, it was unthinkable that anyone could make a beautiful garden in such wind-swept, barren countryside, in the county to which Oliver Cromwell banished many Irish people with the cry "to hell or to Connaught." Lorna's skill consists of making the lay of the land work for her – and in making gardening fun. The garden gives a clear picture of its owner. Memories of the people and the places she loves are interwoven with the plants and with the sites all through the valley that she has cleared. Lorna has made so intimate a mark on the landscape that the garden is as much an expression of the gardener as artist as a painting or piece of sculpture might be.

Above: When Lorna came to Ardcarraig, this was a wild rushy place. Now she can relax, because the plants look after themselves and sometimes combine in an unexpected kaleidoscope.

Plan of Ardcarraig

1. Front Garden
2. Herb Garden
3. Madden Garden
4. Mary O'Conor Garden
5. Primula Garden
6. Bog Garden
7. Stream
8. First Japanese Section
9. Main Japanese Section
10. Harry's Garden
11. Oak Garden
12. Sunken Garden

BALLINLOUGH CASTLE
COUNTY WESTMEATH

Lichen-encrusted eighteenth-century carved stone gateposts opening onto empty fields in the Irish countryside are often all that remain of once prosperous estates. After the end of a family's life on an estate, the houses were sometimes burned out or abandoned. The Land Commission would then buy the land at a nominal price and redistribute it in small acreages to neighboring farmers. The story of Ballinlough Castle and gardens might have been one of abandonment and neglect. After Sir Charles Nugent's death in 1927, the land was parceled out, and the Commission was about to demolish the castle. However, in 1930 Sir Charles' grandson, Hugh, regained some land and the castle from them and he returned with Lady Nugent to restore Ballinlough in 1938. The gateposts that greet today's visitor, topped with urns and hung with fine wrought-iron gates, open onto a long, winding avenue. The castle sits "on a shoulder of bright gleaming grass" and the glassy lake is surrounded by reeds.

*Previous page, main picture: The border of
French lavender occasionally entwined with
old-fashioned roses leads to the wooden gate that
was copied from the one at Highgrove. Through
it, we can glimpse the young beech hedge next to
the magnolia walk in the main walled garden.*

*Previous page, detail: Purple tufted heads
of French lavender (Lavandula stoechas).*

*Above: Pure white foxgloves (Digitalis purpurea
f. albiflora), one of Ireland's most beautiful
native flowers, will seed themselves and spread.*

*Above right: Pepe's favorite old roses with
lilies in a lavender border fill one of the
smaller walled gardens.*

Sir Hugh and Lady Nugent had the huge and complicated job of
retrieving the land and restoring the castle, gardens, and woods. During the
1930s, 1940s, and 1950s, they were able to bring the castle back to being
one of the most picturesque and varied in North Leinster, with its gothic
detailing, curved cornices, paneled hall filled with ancestral portraits, carved
staircase and gallery, and tall rooms with beautiful mantelpieces. The gardens
had become completely overgrown, and Lady Nugent put the first trowel for
about 20 years into the ground in 1940. Probably her greatest achievement
was to unearth the basic pattern of the paths. Following her husband's death
in 1983, she retired to live abroad, and five years later their son John and his
wife Pepe (short for Penelope) came to live here.

Today the whole garden is restored, including the Water Garden which
was rediscovered in 1940. Each compartment in the Walled Garden is like a
jewel box filled with plants. Going away from the eighteenth-century stabled
courtyard, you pass a bed filled with bluebells, hostas, and Iceland poppies
and a wall with cobbled trim made from large river-washed stones. In the
Fruit Garden, cordoned and espaliered fruit trees are neatly planted, and an
octagonal fruit cage is being built to save the soft fruit from being devoured
by birds. Medlars, damsons, apples, pears, mulberries, greengages, and plums
grow trained on the walls and in rows across the grass.

Two huge, colorful perennial beds run the length of each side of the
dividing path in the main Walled Garden. A collection of pink and yellow
epimediums flourishes near the entrance arch, and the wall at the other end is
covered by a trained wisteria, with rows of Guernsey lilies that flower in fall. A
magnolia walk along a beech hedge leads to a gothic gate, copied from one in
the Prince of Wales's garden at Highgrove, through which you can see the

Rose Garden. A border of French lavender leads down the center, while old-fashioned roses line the borders along the walls with the pinks and crimsons in one corner, champagnes and creams in another.

A lovely walk can be taken from the gardens down to the canal and back through flowerbeds threaded along its banks. This area was cleared and the old rock garden dug out, and primulas, rodgersia, astilbes, and crocosmia planted. Honeysuckle covers the mossy rustic stonework of the old Honeysuckle Bridge, which is made from large, irregular rocks, deliberately arranged in a seemingly random manner. It is similar to the rustic bridge at Danesmote House near Rathfarnham, County Dublin, and to Thomas Wright's rustic bridge at Belvedere, also in County Westmeath. Amid trees and open countryside, the canal provides a beautiful setting for the planting along the bank. A Heather Garden is being established to include the red bell heather *Erica cinerea* 'Kerry Cherry,' found in the wild at Leaghillaun, County Kerry, by the late Sir Hugh.

The restoration of the gardens at Ballinlough has been aided to a large extent by a number of projects and interested individuals. The Nugents were among the first to join the Great Gardens of Ireland Restoration Programme,

Below: Broad, colorful perennial beds have been notable features of Irish gardens for the past century, so it is good to see them flourishing again in gardens like Ballinlough Castle.

Above: A small wooden rowing boat sits by the tranquil lake.

Right: Viewed from across the lake, Ballinlough Castle sits surrounded by the trees of the nineteenth-century park, the walled gardens hidden from view as in many Irish gardens.

spearheaded by Finola Reid, whereby the European Regional Development Fund provides grants to match the amount contributed by the owners of the gardens. Once the restoration is completed, the agreement is that the gardens are then opened to the public. Ursula Walsh, a student of Landscape Horticulture at University College, Dublin, who was writing a thesis on the successful restoration of the historic landscape and gardens was introduced to the Nugents by Finola Reid. Ursula was so fascinated by Ballinlough that, after graduation, she accepted the post of head gardener and has been enthusiastically involved in the whole project ever since.

Finola says that the greatest compliment she can receive after months of work is when people say, "But I don't see what you've been doing; it all looks just like it was." The demesnes go back so far through Irish history and yet survive. She thinks the situation can be compared with that in Russia, the Czech Republic, and other Eastern European countries. For many years it was not "the done thing" in Ireland to be a gardener: gardening was just for the middle class and "elite." Now the perception of gardening has changed, and the whole country is not only middle class but also fiercely garden-minded – all just in time to save these magical places from oblivion.

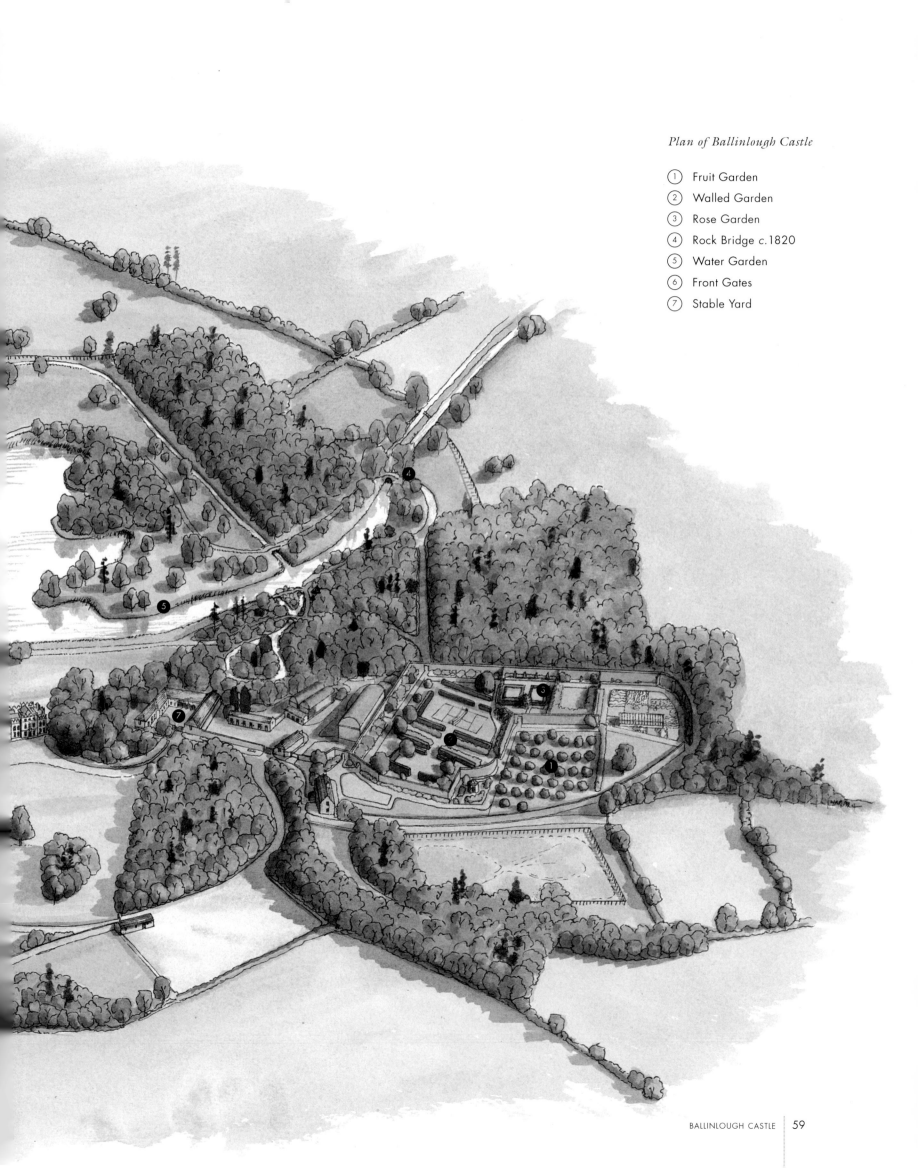

Plan of Ballinlough Castle

1. Fruit Garden
2. Walled Garden
3. Rose Garden
4. Rock Bridge *c.*1820
5. Water Garden
6. Front Gates
7. Stable Yard

BALLYMALOE COOKERY SCHOOL GARDENS
COUNTY CORK

This garden belongs to someone who has been responsible for changing the way an entire Irish generation thinks about food, the sources of food, and the countryside. Darina and Timmy Allen are the daughter-in-law and eldest son of Myrtle Allen, who, with her fruit-farmer husband Ivan, started the nearby Ballymaloe House Hotel and Restaurant in the 1960s, in their eighteenth-century house that is joined onto a medieval tower in the middle of the County Cork countryside.

Myrtle passionately believes that Irish ingredients are among the best in the world and has consistently produced sumptuous food in the Irish country-house tradition. When she was a child, every big house and farm had its own vegetable garden, and she, in turn, uses only homegrown vegetables and local produce in her cooking. Her *Ballymaloe Cookery Book* totally banished the image of Irish food being about overboiled cabbage and greasy lamb chops.

The revolution continues with Darina and Timmy, who started the Ballymaloe Cookery School in a converted farm building near their house at Kinoith in 1983. The school has expanded into the old apple store, where most of the teaching takes place, with the Garden Café and Shop next door.

An early-nineteenth-century house, Kinoith was built along the generous lines of Ireland's Regency period and is surrounded by apple orchards. The bones of the old, much smaller garden can still be seen today – it has simply expanded to meet the growing needs of both the cooking school and hotel. There are now substantial vegetable, fruit, and herb gardens between its high hedges, as well as other gardens not on a strictly culinary theme, such as a the Maze, the Pleasure Garden and the perennial beds.

In the mid-1990s Darina secretly started work on the Shell House, which was to be a surprise 25th-wedding-anniversary present for Timmy. This was

also to be the focal point of a whole new garden. The Shell House originally stood alone in the center of an empty field. Now two straight perennial beds 15 x 328 feet long, designed by Rachel Lamb, lead from the old garden along a green path toward the small closed building. The beds are planted with bronze fennel, day lilies, montbretia, delphiniums, margarita daisies, bellflowers, violets, acanthus, and mallow, all woven into a vivid tapestry. This part of the garden is not yet mature, but it is fascinating to see it in its early stages, reminding us that the mature gardens we see today looked like this to the people who began them, and it brings home the huge amount of planning and hard work that goes into the carving up of a field to make a garden.

The tradition of Irish shell houses goes back to the eighteenth century, to Mrs. Delany and her contemporaries. There is a particularly beautiful one at Larchill in County Kildare and the famous Shell Cottage at Carton, also in

Previous page, main picture: Cloches modeled on Victorian originals, made by Isaac, Darina and Timmy's eldest son, help this remarkable organic potager produce vegetables all year round.

Previous page, detail: Withy scarecrow guarding the Kitchen Garden.

Above: The inspiration for the Herb Garden was Château Villandry. Like every good garden plan, the original sketch was made by Darina on the back of an envelope.

Opposite: Long ago, this lead waterbarrow was actually used.

County Kildare, decorated by Emily, Duchess of Leinster, on the death of her son, Lord Edward FitzGerald. The modest appearance of the octagonal building at Kinoith offers no clue as to the dazzling interior within. Shells had been collected by family and friends from beaches all around the coast of Ireland and saved from the school and restaurant. Charlotte Kerr-Wilson, known as Blot, an artist who specializes in shell work, came over from England to work on this secret project. With help from the Allen children, Blot began by washing the treasures she had brought with her, such as abalone shells and coral. She also suggested that the old Irish roof slates should have one end rounded off so they looked like fish scales.

She first drew her ideas on the walls in chalk and then stuck the precious shells on top. The popularity of the seafood platter in the Ballymaloe restaurant is very much in evidence in the bands and swirls of scallops, mussels, cockles, and oyster shells, while the humbler periwinkle is used as edging. Every surface is tightly covered with shells, so not a sliver of wall is visible. The floor of the Shell House is made of pebbles; and outside, rivulets of pebbles have been set into the surrounding pavement. Candles are often set down here in the evening.

To the right of the borders stands the yew Maze, which was designed by Peter Lamb and Lesey Beck in a celtic pattern and planted in 1997. The yews have not yet reached the desired impenetrability – they have a few more years' growth yet. It is fitting that there is a maze in the garden at the school since mazes are a symbol of man's quest for truth and enlightenment.

Back up the path to the left of the house is the old garden, which is believed to date back to the 1840s. It is known as Lydia's Garden, after Lydia Strangman, who persuaded her father to build her a summerhouse there in 1912. The floor was laid with the ceramic chips of broken blue, white, and pink kitchen china in the shape of a shamrock, rose, and thistle. In 1972 this part of the old garden was totally overrun by weeds. The Allens cut back the antique beech hedge, then entangled with briars and ivy, and planted the beds around the lawns with roses and asters, penstemons and mallow, pinks and lavender, and with holly and laurel for shelter. The rustic Tree House was then built beyond the little pool. Wooden stairs take you to the platform, which is entwined with roses, honeysuckle, and clematis. From here you can see the surrounding countryside and the perennial beds that stretch to the Shell House, as well as the specimen trees and pond in the Pleasure Garden, and the Herb Garden on the other side of the high beech hedge.

Having been inspired by her visit to the potager and herb gardens at the Château de Villandry, in the Loire Valley, Darina's Herb Garden contains every conceivable culinary and medicinal herb. The herbs include rosemary, thyme, blue-leaved sage, lemon balm, lemon verbena, garlic chives, tarragon, comfrey, hyssop, evening primrose, camphor, different kinds of sorrel, as well as lots of different mints such as applemint, ginger mint, eau-de-cologne mint, and spearmint. The herbs are planted in medieval-patterned beds set among

Above: Bees enjoying the nectar from the round heads of the globe thistle.

Opposite: Silver and blue with a splash of orange in one of the new beds that lead you toward a mysterious small garden building.

gravel and enclosed by boxwood. There is a beech exedra at one end of the plot and a gazebo at the other. Among the herbs are edible flowers, such as violas and marigolds, which are also gathered every day by students and gardeners at Ballymaloe. Also here are sea-kale plants, whose leaves are forced into succulent whiteness under terracotta pots with lids. The Herb Garden is the heart and soul of the gardens at Ballymaloe, and the part that has made the greatest impression on garden visitors over the years.

The compartment next to the Herb Garden was an impenetrable thicket before Darina cleared it away and planted a lawn with specimen trees. In spring the cherry and apple trees bloom and out come the dark red bells on the Crinodendron and the fluffy scarlet flowers of the Australian bottlebrush. There is a pond and a temple made from pillars rescued from a demolished house in Kilkenny, all sheltered by a line of ancient beech.

The Kitchen Garden was finished in 1993. The soil here is excellent since it had been used as a dump for mushroom compost for many years. It is sheltered by a little wood, and the path through this to the Kitchen Garden is always occupied by hens. Diamond-shaped boxwood parterres are filled with seasonal vegetables, and other beds are edged with frills of flowers, such as orange and yellow nasturtiums, edible marigolds and chrysanthemums, violas, bachelor's buttons and purple catnip. Four clipped standard bay balls stand in the center of the beds and a spiral of twisted boxwood in the middle of the herringbone brick paths. The vegetables are rotated each year within the beds according to the planned crop rotation system. An extraordinary mixture of vegetables is ready each day for seasonal picking. Beans of various kinds, peas, ruby chard, every sort of lettuce, spinach, Greek cress, radicchio, orach, broccoli, curly kale, pumpkins, globe artichokes, corn salad, lamb's lettuce, corn, asparagus, radishes, and Chinese cabbage are all grown in succession, overseen by a beaming fringe of golden sunflowers at the top of the patch. Seven varieties of tomato are grown in the greenhouse.

Next to the school is the formal Fruit Garden, designed by Jim Reynolds. The students can sit on the wide steps in summer and see the fruit ripening before their eyes. Against the walls are fan-trained peaches and apricots, pears, an almond tree, pink and yellow and summer- and fall-fruiting raspberries, tayberries, and loganberries, several mulberries, gooseberries, wine berries, and black, red, and white currants, greengages, plums, an olive tree, and old Irish apple trees trained over arches. These Irish varieties of apples have been rescued from old orchards and walled gardens all over the country.

This is a garden that has evolved organically and has an aura of vitality. Darina Allen is an inspiring and dedicated teacher, and with her interest in garden design it is inevitable that she will create more gardens as her plans evolve. But despite its constant evolution, this garden has not lost its connection with the past – the atmosphere of the quiet Edwardian garden that once stood behind its enclosed hedges in the middle of apple orchards is still there, but running through it is a buzz of modern excitement and purpose.

Above: The shells that decorate the walls of the Shell House came from local beaches or from the school and hotel kitchens.

Opposite: Roses and swirls and ribbons of shells smother the inside of the mysterious small building – Darina's inspired present for Timmy.

Proposed Plan of Ballymaloe Cookery School Gardens

1. Tree house
2. Rose Garden
3. Provencal Allée
4. Shell House
5. Irish Apple Meadow
6. Maze
7. Green Garden
8. Wilderness and Pool
9. Pool and Temple
10. Pleasure Garden
11. Ornamental Fowl
12. Fruit Garden
13. Herb Garden
14. Lydia's Garden
15. Kitchen Garden

BIRR CASTLE
COUNTY OFFALY

The gothic baronial pile of Birr Castle has been home to the Parsons family, later the Earls of Rosse, since 1620. The fortified castle stands in its 150-acre demesne, in the middle of Ireland, on a dramatic site perched over the sparkling River Camcor as it flows through the wooded valley. The roofs of the town of Birr cluster around its walls.

The gardens exude an atmosphere of tranquility, and to wander through them is a soothing experience. Birr is a fine example of a landscape park with an artificial lake, and unlike many similar landscape gardens in Ireland, it has had a continuous program of new planting since the 1930s. The trees are mature, and the planting is so graceful that the overall impression of the gardens is one of light and space. Over the centuries, the castle and townspeople have always been interdependent, and over the last two generations, members of the Parsons family have been especially gifted and particularly knowledgeable gardeners.

Previous page, main picture: The honeysuckle covering this stone wall is Lonicera etrusca *'Michael Rosse,' named after the present Earl of Rosse's father.*

Previous page, detail: The remarkable sloe-colored cones produced by George Forrest's fir (Abies forrestii).

Above: Elegant stone urns are ideal focal points in the Formal Gardens.

Above right: The allées *of hornbeam with arched and interwoven branches are tunnels of green in midsummer.*

When the Parsons came here, having conquered the O'Carrolls in the seventeenth century, there are accounts of their chopping down an orchard and buying new fruit trees. A recipe book from that time has a list of many herbal remedies, as well as a recipe for "hartichoke pie" made from Jerusalem artichokes grown in the castle's walled kitchen gardens, which still exist today.

It was Sir Laurence Parsons' grandson, the second Earl of Rosse, who gave the castle the appearance that we see today. He turned the house away from facing the town and "gothicized" the front directly opposite the park. In 1810, he spanned the river with one of the earliest surviving suspension bridges. His son, William, third Earl of Rosse, became one of the most distinguished astronomers of the nineteenth century and built in Birr what was the largest reflecting telescope in the world. His wife, Mary, was a Yorkshire heiress, and it was her fortune that enabled him to carry out so many "improvements." In addition, he had built a series of Vaubanesque fortifications, which provided employment and relief during the Famine. Unfortunately, much of his planting went unrecorded. However, his splendid giant redwood still exists, as does the fernery planted by the countess.

The present earl's grandfather, the fifth Earl, started gardening in 1908, but only had six years at home before going off to fight in World War I. By leveling part of the moat, he and his wife, Lois, created the terraces built up from the river to the west of the castle. They also started the Formal Gardens and planted the first magnolias. The fifth Earl was in correspondence with Augustine Henry, the Irishman who had made collections of plants in China in the late 1880s and who inspired his son Michael to become a botanist.

Michael, the sixth Earl of Rosse, who succeeded to the title in 1918 after his father was killed in action, acquired an encyclopedic knowledge of botany. He also corresponded with Chinese botanists and organized key plant-hunting expeditions in China, including Tse-Tsun Yu's expedition to remote parts of western China. Today, many of the seedlings raised from Yu's seed are mature trees and shrubs at Birr. The archive records reveal Michael's 10 shillings' worth of shares in the Kingdon Ward expedition to China, with the dividend payable in seeds. He also collected plants and seeds on his own trips to places such as Mexico and Tibet. The result is that Birr Castle contains one of the most important collections of woody plants in Ireland, many of which were raised from seeds collected in the wild. The fact that the collections were of such scientific importance prompted Michael Rosse to invite the Heritage Gardens Committee of An Taisce (the Irish National Trust) to catalog the trees and shrubs, a project that was undertaken by Mary Forrest with the support of the National Botanic Gardens, Glasnevin. Michael was also known for his generosity in liberally distributing plants to other Irish gardens.

Below: Viewed through one of the "windows" in the allée, *pyramids and scrolls of clipped box recreate the style of gardening fashionable in the eighteenth century.*

Above: Birr Castle stands at the end of one of the vistas through the eighteenth Century park. On the right is "Lord Rosse's Leviathan," the great telescope.

In 1935, he married Anne, the daughter of Leonard Messel, who had created the famous garden at Nymans in Sussex, England, and it was in their care that the demesne really came into its own. Messel's grandson, the present earl, remembers that one of his favorite sayings was "a penny for a plant and a pound for the planting." The gardens at Birr today are formally "twinned" with Nymans so as to ensure the continuing exchange of plants, as well as visits to each other's gardens by the head gardeners. The late Anne, Countess of Rosse, was a most intelligent gardener, with great artistic gifts, and it was really her feeling for design and her "painterly eye" that gave rise to the sense

of visual satisfaction gained from looking at the sweep of Brownian landscape down to the lake. To celebrate their marriage, she designed the pleached hornbeam cloisters edged with ribbons of snowdrops in the Formal Gardens. The square of baroque tunnels has a filigree of branches carefully espaliered and then trained to curve and entwine at the top. Cut into the leafy walls are windows, through which you can see a pair of stone urns from Bavaria standing in the middle of the boxwood parterre. There are also boxwood obelisks at each corner. Statues of the Graces sheltered by rose-enclosed arbors can be seen at one end of the leafy tunnels, and the pink petals of

Above: The lake was created by damming the River Camcor in the late eighteenth century. Wild sedge and rushes and other plants characteristic of marshy places have colonized the shore line.

Top: The pure-white blossoms of this magnolia stand out on leafless branches against the sparkling River Camcor and the vivid green of its grassy banks.

Above: Magnolias are one of the special attractions of Birr Castle, flowering from the beginning of spring.

Magnolia 'Michael Rosse' beckon you to the other. There is a backing of thick yew hedge on one side, with a bed still retaining many of the original plants, including yellow day lilies, peonies, and an edging of catnip. Against the wall is a lush perennial bed containing single, double, and semidouble purple, white, and blue delphinium hybrids, in the middle of which is the white-painted garden seat that Anne designed with their initials intertwined to form the back. Magnolias flourish in the long grass, in a row on the lawn opposite.

Walking down from the castle in the spring past the terraces and seeing a cloud of blossoms ahead, it is exciting to realize that so many plants have been named after members of the family, including the magnolias 'Anne Rosse' and 'Leonard Messel,' *Camellia* 'Leonard Messel,' *Paeonia* 'Anne Rosse,' and even a honeysuckle, *Lonicera etrusca* 'Michael Rosse.' The gardens at Birr certainly demonstrate that it is a fallacy to think magnolias cannot be grown in lime. In fact, they positively thrive, especially down by the River Camcor, where a quilt of blue-eyed Mary (*Omphalodes cappadocica*) covers the ground around their feet. Anne Rosse had found these celestial-blue flowers growing in a solid carpet under an avenue of trees in an exquisite garden in the nearby demesne of a Carolean house called Gloster. They seem to be more vigorous and have larger, bluer flowers than the forms cultivated in England, and it is thought that they could be an old Irish cultivar, which had been "lost" and then "found" again. Another jewellike Irish garden variety at Birr is the ravishing *Omphalodes cappadocica* 'Starry Eyes,' which has a white eye in the center of blue petals, rimmed with pale mauve, and a darker blue central flash.

Kowhai (*Sophora tetraptera*) from New Zealand, with its mustard-yellow blossom, spreads itself across the gray stone of the castle walls. Looking back through a clearing, the pink flowers of *Magnolia dawsoniana* and *M.* x *veitchii*

*Above left: The burgeoning young leaves of the giant Chilean rhubarb (*Gunnera mannicata*) will eventually be 6 feet high and spread like umbrellas.*

Right: The flower spikes, like golden cones, of Gunnera mannicata *are often 2 feet tall.*

stand out against the background of dark green conifers and the glittering river. A trimmed hedge of flowering quince edges the Terrace Walk, where the huge *Magnolia delavayi*, with gray-green leaves, was supplied by the Veitch nursery just before World War I. Ahead of you stands what is reputed to be the largest gray poplar in the world, with its roots stretching down toward the widening, rushing river.

In spring, hundreds of aconites and daffodils spread under the trees by the river. At the small Stone Bridge, the River Brosna meets the River Camcor, with the lake on one side and the river on the other. Strange and mysterious sluices hidden among laurels, boxwood, and wild violets are controlled by elaborate nineteenth-century machinery, and a channel of the river is tied into a clever knot and then whirled underground and out into the lake beyond. During the eighteenth century, the river used to run through the lake, and it is the head race that goes under the path. A weeping willow is reflected in the water, and sometimes you can see a swan swimming through the reeds. A pale pink October cherry (*Prunus subhirtella*) is planted in contrast to the holm oak (*Quercus ilex*) leaning over the bridge, and from anywhere in the park you can see the three gold willows (*Salix alba* 'Britzensis') standing next to a slash of orange barberry and the eighteenth-century beech trees.

Across the bridge, you walk through a tunnel of bamboo, so curved and with such crisp edges that it feels as if you are in a modern building. You emerge into a fairyland vista opposite the castle, with the branches of a *Magnolia kobus* framing the flowery banks across the river. In spring the giant Chilean rhubarb (*Gunnera manicata*) begins to unfold, and a dark green Monterey cypress (*Cupressus macrocarpa*) stands in a field of fritillaries. Ducks fly upstream, and the park is alight with magnolias. Looking back

Above: The brick bridge over the River Camcor.
Nearby, three counties – Tipperary, Offaly, and
Roscommon – meet within the demesne.

across the water you can see purple aubrieta stream down the high stone wall
holding up the castle side of the river, with the thin suspension bridge
balanced delicately from bank to bank.

As you turn back on yourself and follow the curve of the river along past
the lake, you reach a small pocket of wild woodland, followed by an avenue of
young cherry trees. On your left is an astonishing huge flowering pear tree,
which looks, in blossom, very much like a white cloud surrounded by seven
huge mounds of very old boxwood. Leaving the lake and the Arboretum
behind, you come to the Fernery, which the "Telescope Earl" and his wife
started work on in 1850 as the last burst of their improvements.

From under the laurels you suddenly see a solid sheet of water tipping
over a sharp-edged rock into a rocky gully with horny tufa walls and dribbling
streams. The stream rushes down the gully, and gravity fuels a hidden
fountain so the water flies up from the riverbed in three spiraling jets. Alison,
the present Countess of Rosse, says that when she first came to live here this
area was completely overgrown, and when the Conservation Volunteers
cleaned out the riverbed they discovered the original blocked fountain pipes.
Ferns grow up the edges of the gorge in a damp microclimate of their own,
which she hopes will suit the two Australian tree ferns (*Dicksonia antartica*)
that she planted there in 1998.

Walking again toward the Formal Gardens, you can see over the wall the candles of magnolia buds in spring, and you come to the nerve center of the demesne. Here are the greenhouses and propagating houses, which fuel all of Birr's planting. Nearby stand two thin rows of boxwood, which have grown and grown, making them, according to the *Guinness Book of Records*, the tallest boxwood hedges in the world. They would have been part of Sir William Parsons' original seventeenth-century garden plan. Ancient yews, apple trees, and romantic roses, such as 'Duchesse de Montebello' and 'Belle Amour,' fill another walled garden, while in a small garden on the side of the greenhouses a vast twisted wisteria embraces an iron support.

Crossing the park by the Meridian Path drawn from the telescope to the Formal Gardens, you pass the linden trees planted by the present earl and countess to commemorate the nebulae discovered by the "Telescope Earl." Beyond the oaks, Manchurian birch, southern beech, and Turkish hazel, you come to the telescope itself, which for so long was the focus of attention throughout the scientific world. With the help of the government and the Ireland Funds, "Lord Rosse's Leviathan" was restored in the 1990s. Around it the Great Gardens of Ireland Restoration Programme is helping to conserve and restore the gardens to their original splendor, illustrating as they do so many different aspects of the fashions and history of Irish gardening.

Above: Springtime – a naturalized drift of daffodils on a slope beside the river, with one of Birr's many magnolias.

Plan of Birr Castle

1. Entrance
2. River Camcor
3. Telescope
4. Meridian Path
5. The Lake
6. Arboretum
7. Brick Bridge
8. Fernery
9. Kitchen Walk
10. Formal Gardens
11. Yew Avenue
12. Orchard

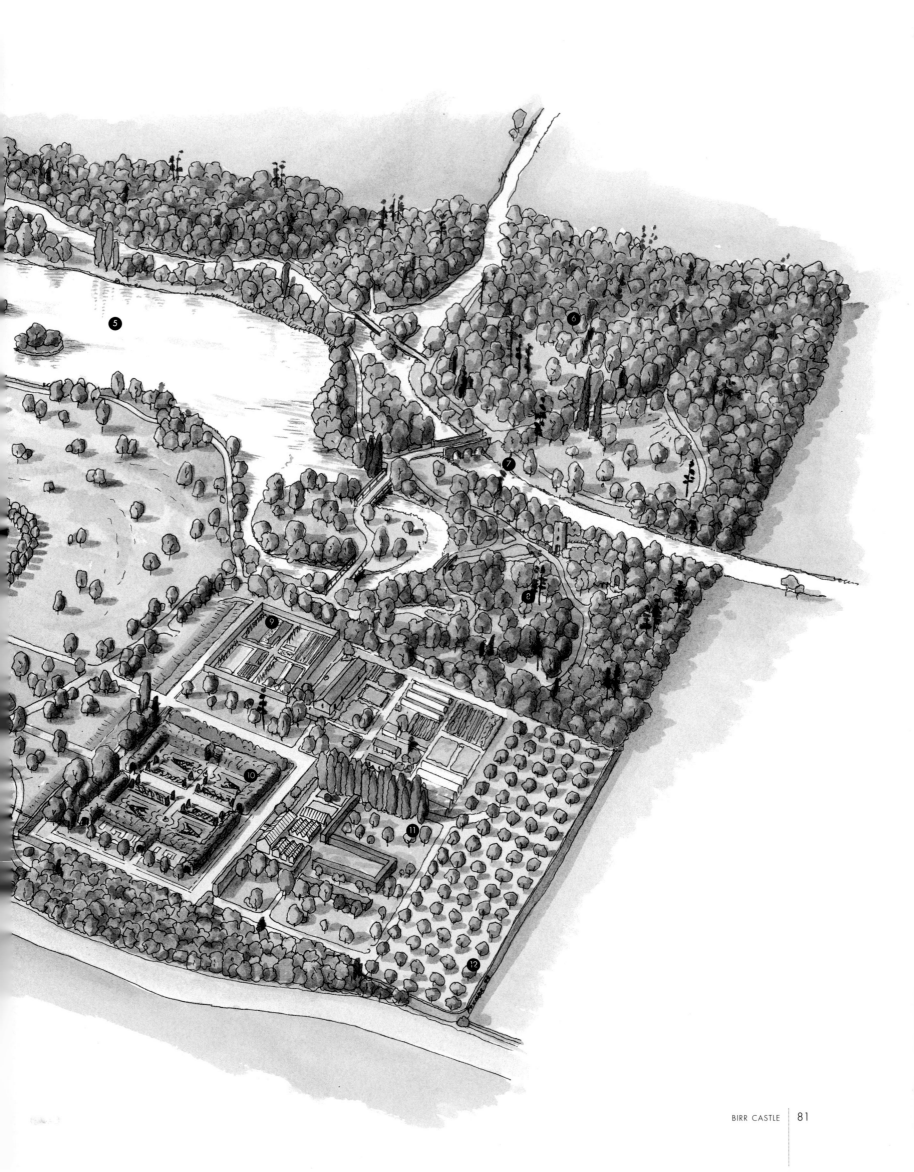

BUTTERSTREAM
COUNTY MEATH

The creation of Butterstream did not follow the conventional Irish formula of grand house and grand garden, with parks, lodges, follies, and grottoes. The owner, Jim Reynolds, had always wanted to have a garden, but, beset by images of traditional demesnes in the surrounding countryside, he couldn't quite see how a garden could work as an entity of its own without the accompanying impressive house. And then, as an archeology student, he visited Sissinghurst, and everything fell into place. Here at last was a garden that didn't follow the norm: rather, Italian Renaissance meets the English countryside, the only building in sight being a Tudor gatehouse. And yet the enclosures, paths, hedges, borders, terraces, and trees all had a life and a logic of their own within the structure of the garden itself. Vita Sackville-West and her husband, Harold Nicolson, had created a garden out of a wilderness – and so could Jim. Life on the Reynolds' family farm in Trim, County Meath, would never be the same again.

Previous page, main picture: The tower that is inspired by a local ruined pigeon house. At its base grow good old-fashioned cottage-garden plants: delphiniums, phloxes, double white sneezewort, and bellflowers.

Previous page, detail: View from the tower.

Jim didn't have much to work with. On one side of the road, there was the busy town of Trim, and on the other a field. And that single field formed the basis of the magical gardens we see today. Armed with spade, shovel, saw, and sledge-hammer, Jim singlehandedly set to work in 1970. He began by fencing off a little bit of the land and planting a beech hedge. The first major task was to drain the relatively low-lying old flood plain. The banks had to be leveled, scrubby hedges dug out, and several farm buildings removed.

Working by now as an archeologist for the Office of Public Works during the day, Jim gardened in the evenings and on the weekends. He thought big, and visited gardens all over Europe in search of inspiration, starting in Ireland, with Birr Castle, Illnacullin, and Mount Stewart. He devoured garden books that came his way, especially ones by his heroine Vita Sackville-West and heroes Lanning Roper and Graham Stuart Thomas. What had started as "an irrational urge to possess a few roses" developed over the years as he

implemented the principles of design, layout, and planting. As his plans became more ambitious, so the parameters of the field widened. "Most of my knowledge," he sighs, "has come, expensively, through experience."

As the garden took shape, Jim began to develop a name for himself within the gardening fraternity and came to the attention of the general public after Sybil Connolly and Helen Dillon included the garden in their book *In an Irish Garden*, in 1986. Since then, Butterstream has become one of the most admired of all modern Irish gardens. Jim wrote a gardening column for the *Irish Times*. He also lectures, makes television appearances, and crisscrosses the county offering advice on garden design and planting. He is chairman of the Great Gardens of Ireland Restoration Programme, where his enormous enthusiasm and knowledge are constantly called upon to encourage others.

Having visited the gardens of Ireland's mild coastal region, Jim, perhaps naively, assumed that he, too, could grow camellias, rhododendrons, Chilean

Above left: View of the Italian Garden with pond and temple. The rose 'Belvedere Rambler,' looking like a pale-pink powder puff, climbs the small square building that came from the late-Georgian gate house at Grangemore, in County Westmeath. Jim bought the building for a song in 1985.

Above: The Italian Garden viewed from the other side of the Liscannor flagstone terrace, showing the five boxwood balls in their earthenware pots. The pool is filled with water lilies.

Above: The dark double-flowered opium poppy comes out in June and, along with peonies and columbines, is one of the early delights of the perennial bed.

firebushes, and all the other Robinsonian delights. He soon learned that the heavy limestone soil and hard winter frosts of the midlands of Ireland are not suitable for what he originally had in mind. So he turned his attention to roses. They are one of the abounding delights of Butterstream. They are given the utmost freedom and, as a result, are everywhere you look, blurring the strict geometry of the layout of the garden. Jim's passion is for the scented old hybrid musk and species roses. He describes the 'Jacques Cartier' rose as being pink and full, opening out flat with an enfolded center. The 'Ferdinand Pichard' rose is a striped pink Bourbon rose; Vita Sackville-West said it was like the "finest claret stirred into whipped cream." 'Madame Hardy' is a lovely flat white rose with a green eye; and 'Céleste,' loose and a delicate shell pink, has the most exquisitely formed small buds of all. 'Madame Alfred Carrière' is a vigorous white climber with a hint of green in her large flowers – "she hurls herself over everything." The delicious pink-cupped 'Belvedere' – which got

Above: The massed seed pods of the poppies are as handsome as the flowers and provide tints of blue and gray. Pale toadflax and tall dark alliums add to this inspired arrangement.

its name because Anne, Countess of Rosse, found it growing in the garden at Belvedere House, on the shore of Lough Ennell, outside Mullingar, County Westmeath – can grow to 40 feet. Graham Stuart Thomas records seeing one cascading out of a holly at Nymans, in Sussex, where it had been grown from a cutting brought over from Ireland.

The entrance to Butterstream, opposite project housing, is quietly informal. A beautiful bower of roses marks the beginning of the garden and has a cottage feel. From here, a winding path leads, in spring, through snowdrops and crocuses and hellebores and pulmonaria, small trees, shrubs, and species roses. This is the romantic end of the garden, with a little gothic bridge leading to a trellis topped with a gilded pineapple. It not only gives the roses and a *Clematis macropetala* support: Jim thinks this construction looks back to past glories. Among the roses is the stunning shell-pink rose 'Souvenir de St. Anne's' (named after Lady Ardilaun's garden in Dublin), at the foot of

which is a forest of opium poppies, foxgloves, alliums, toadflax, self-seeding feverfew, and cranesbill. The scent of old-fashioned roses and different mock orange (*Philadelphus*) fills the air, contributing a vital element to the garden. A ground cover of ferns and the pretty candelabra primrose 'Lissadell Pink,' which was raised in the wonderful nursery at Lissadell in the 1930s, gives way to edgings of rippling green hostas as you approach the stream. Jim firmly believes that gardening should be a relaxing and enjoyable pursuit, and urges you not to worry if you haven't sprayed the roses, or if the slugs are eating the hostas. Rather, he says, nature can't always be pristine and shining, and you should look up rather than down during the garden tour.

The walls of the outdoor "rooms" are made of hedges, which provide shelter from the cold in winter and protection from the drying winds that cross the steppes of County Meath in summer. The original three "rooms" have expanded to 15, with a collection of connecting anterooms, corridors, and stairways. Each "room" acts as a showcase for its own particular garden idea, and yet all lock together in perfect synchronicity.

The Green Walk, flanked by contrasting foliage, leads to the enclosure filled, seasonally, with hot oranges and reds through to bronzes and golds. The scarlet *Dahlia* 'Bishop of Llandaff,' red and yellow tulips, and orange oriental poppies, the fiery red *Crocosmia* 'Lucifer,' the golden false acacia (*Robinia pseudoacacia* 'Frisia'), bronze New Zealand flaxes, and a bronze cabbage-palm (*Cordyline*) sizzle together, hemmed in by a high hedge.

Walking on through a green opening, you enter another section, dedicated to old-fashioned Damask, Gallica, Bourbon, and Moss roses. In midsummer, if you climb to the top of the tower inspired by a local ruined pigeon-house, you look down onto a wave of crimson, pink, and white roses breaking and frothing over the top of the green walls, which only just prevent them from clambering into the White Garden next door.

The White Garden is made up of four squares, divided by paths and clipped hedges. Depending on the time of year, there are bellflowers, peonies, the famous and desirable Chinese tree peony 'Joseph Rock,' and lots of white tulips. White toadflax arrives early in the year, followed by *Hydrangea arborescens* 'Annabelle,' many white roses, double white sneezewort (*Achillea ptarmica* 'The Pearl'), white goat's rue (*Galega*), clouds of phlox mixed with silver foliage plants, and variegated grasses. Tall cardoons add height and architectural form. The main passageway is clipped in layers; and down the center run five pairs of terracotta pots filled with white margarita daisies, sunk into the wide hedges standing on each side of the path, in their own carved outer pots of boxwood. "From up in the tower," says Jim with satisfaction, "you can see the very straight lines of the hedges with mad confusion inside."

Just beyond the White Garden, you catch a glimpse of the wild profusion of the perennial beds. These are a series of deep beds interwoven with curving grass paths. In springtime there are lots of tulips, and then the various networks of herbaceous plants start to develop. In late spring, there are opium poppies, peonies, and columbines, mixed with sweet rocket; and then the first delphiniums appear, accompanied by most types of bellflower – in blue, mauve, and pink – and finally the delicious little red scabious *Knautia macedonica*. In contrast to the early colors – pale yellows mixed with blue, pink, and silver, which Jim can find "a bit boudoirish" – the late summer sees stronger colors: the old-fashioned varieties of phlox, followed by hemp agrimony (*Eupatorium*), goat's rues, loosestrifes (*Lythrum*), lobelias, and Japanese anemones. The strident yellow and purple of the two meadow rues (*Thalictrum lucidum* and *T. delavayi*) and the perennial sunflowers are set against the lovely yellow-cream herbaceous *Potentilla recta* var. *pallida*.

Leaving the perennial beds, you come across an elegant sundial, bought from a traveler in 1976. In this room, the white climbing rose 'Kiftsgate' grows alongside the sturdy cream-colored 'Rambling Rector,' which was first included in the Daisy Hill Nursery catalog in 1912. The 'Sanders White Rambler' tumbles over the wall, and banks of milky bellflower (*Campanula lactiflora*) are punctuated by the spikes of delphiniums.

Walking through the Laburnum Tunnel, you come to the Obelisk Garden, which Jim started after an ash tree blew down, annihilating a greenhouse. Bridget Ordway of Blackcastle had given him 14 boxwood plants, which he clipped into little pyramids and set into gravel in a square formation, adding a

Top: Corners of the White Garden with margarita daisies in pots and milky bellflowers.

Above: Part of Jim's "mad confusion" of herbaceous plants: white rosebay willowherb with masterwort, bellflowers, and meadow rue.

Above: Illusions of grandeur – the canals and pavilions were built from scratch a few years ago in what was an open field.

larger clipped obelisk in the center. One side is his "seven virtues," and the other side his "seven deadly sins." The idea for this garden came to Jim as he was lying in bed thinking of the Piranesi print of the Circus Maximus.

Across the laurel lawn, you come to the Pool Garden, an evocation of a villa garden in Pompeii, which houses a small Tuscan square temple. On the flagstone terrace, earthenware pots are filled with boxwood. Mock orange blossoms hang over the pillars of the temple, and white willowherb grows in the space beyond. There are water lilies in the pool, and the rose 'Belvedere Rambler,' climbs over the pergola. This compartment seems to be the finale of the journey through the garden – but if you press on, you find a little secret path under two old trees that leads to an airy lawned area. On each side of the lawn is a small temple covered with winding clematis. Growing around are Musk roses, shrubs, lots of cranesbills, and the mop-headed false acacia, as well as the sycamore *Acer pseudoplatanus* 'Brilliantissimum,' which has leaves

Below: Evening light on a gothic bridge, one of Jim Reynolds' many formal embellishments at Butterstream.

stained shrimp-pink and apricot in spring. The stone doorway that was salvaged from an eighteenth-century house in Trim, owned by Lord Mornington, is set into the wall that leads through a terrace to the pavilions built on each side. These, Jim admits, were an act of folly, but he couldn't resist trying to capture the essence of the 1750s. The pavilions do not block any view in the garden. From their Venetian windows you see two canals, at the end of which grass steps lead to a pair of seats.

After a delicious tea, you then wend your way home, leaving via what Jim calls the Vegetable Department. Peas, beans, seakale, and artichokes grow in a formal design of a little avenue of seven high boxwood obelisks. Old-fashioned iron arbors have Irish varieties of apples trained over them to show off their blossoms and fruit. On the way out, you might perhaps buy Lady Ardilaun's vigorous shell-pink Edwardian rose 'Souvenir de St. Anne's,' in memory of a gentle wasp-waisted garden enthusiast of long ago.

Plan of Butterstream

1. Kitchen Garden
2. Stream
3. Gothic Bridge
4. Green Walk
5. Hot Coloured Garden
6. Tower & Blue Garden
7. White Garden
8. Herbaceous Borders
9. Laburnum Tunnel
10. Obelisk Garden
11. Italian Garden
12. Lawn & Summer House
13. Pavilions
14. Lime Allées & Canals

CREAGH

COUNTY CORK

Creagh's garden has been planted on the edge of the water, where the river runs into the sea between the towns of Baltimore and Skibbereen on the western coast of County Cork. From the house you can see the small and verdant island of Inisbeg in the distance. It is a wild and unruly garden with a romantic atmosphere, with two sides of the planting hemmed in by the seawall and the shore.

The garden at Creagh is the life's work of a passionate gardener, the late Peter Harold-Barry. In 1937, Peter, from Ballyvonaire outside Buttevant in County Cork, married Gwendoline, the daughter of Sir Edmund Browne and his French wife. They had originally met as children in Youghal and were reacquainted in England, where they were to marry in Westminster Cathedral. After World War II, they returned to Ireland and bought Creagh as their family home. It was a happy and comfortable home that was always filled with interesting guests.

Previous page, main picture: A mossy tanglewood of beech and wild bluebells.

Previous page, detail: Raindrops on a flat yellow umbel of fennel.

Above: The view looking back towards the garden from the pebbled beach of the seashore, with the tall Monterey pines of Sir John's Walk clearly visible, and the distant church nearly hidden by trees.

Opposite: Sir John's Walk – an avenue of Monterey pines, which can thrive even on the windswept coast. Monterey pine is now very rare in the wild, but it is one of the most useful trees for sheltering seaside gardens.

In the winter, Peter and Gwen would retire to their house in Dublin, where they had many friends, among whom were writers such as Mary Lavin and the famous genealogist and broadcaster Pope O'Mahony. In 1963, however, their peaceful lives were shattered by the death of their daughter, Christina, in a car accident. Gwen became a recluse and remained so until she died, while Peter, though still cheerful, devoted himself ever more to the garden. Until a few months before his death in 1994, he was still planting new plants and looking at others as old friends. Peter had begun opening the gardens to the public and used to leave a small bucket on the front porch as an "honesty box" into which visitors put their entrance money.

With the shoreline washed by the waves of the Gulf Stream, the growth in the garden is almost tropical. Peter's inspiration for the garden came from the paintings of the nineteenth-century French primitive painter Henri Rousseau, known as Le Douanier; the plant picture that he succeeded in creating is exactly the sort of exotic environment in which one of Rousseau's tigers might glare out from the prickly fronds. Essentially it is a wild garden in which plants have been allowed to become naturalized. They are not held in check except to make sure they do not overwhelm their neighbors, which is the essence of the wild garden promoted by William Robinson. At Creagh, the mild and moist climate means that, as long as shelter is provided against storms and gales, subtropical species will thrive, and it can accommodate really exotic plants.

Peter's beloved tender fuchsias were planted against the dry stone walls of the grass-covered terrace that he built at the back of the house. This overlooks the sweep of the lawn ringed by trees and shrubs, on which fêtes, plays, and charity open days are staged during the summer. A stone-flagged bridge leads into a wood with giant Chilean rhubarb and huge-leaved rhododendrons to left and right. Moving deeper into the wood, you pass azaleas, camellias, and more rhododendrons. Farther on, around a corner, in spring there is a superb carpet of bluebells, which are sheltered behind a hedge under the Scots pines. Ferns push up through the moss, and camellias are mixed with holly and escallonia. A field of Friesian cows completes the pastoral scene. Along the Fern Walk, past the donkeys in Malachy's Field, you finally reach the Boat House, with its seaweed-covered slip built from slices of slate and sheltered by a fringe of wind-torn hazel. The triangle of meeting waters formed by the deep river constantly flowing into the tidal seabed can be seen from different angles through the cuts in the seawall. Here, the Harold-Barrys used to board their launch to do the shopping in nearby Skibbereen, and the moss-covered, deformed branches of an ancient beech still form a comfortable seat.

A small iron gate leads out of the wood and along the springy turf of Sir John's Walk, named after Sir John Wrixon-Becher, a former owner of the garden. The whistling wind can be heard in the treetops of the double avenue of huge Monterey pines (*Pinus radiata*) parallel to the shore. You emerge into the prettiest and most delicate woodland dotted with pale-pink rhododendrons, flame-colored Chilean firebushes (*Embothrium coccineum*),

Above: The neatly constructed hen house, made from logs, was influenced by the style of a Czechoslovakian mountain hut and put up in the walled garden in 1992.

Right: Salad greens and herbs – with leeks, clipped box, and a background of fennel – in the walled vegetable garden.

and *Magnolia* x *soulangeana*, its delicate white flowers flushed with pink. From a tunnel of laurel trees, you sometimes catch a glimpse of the water, but otherwise you walk completely covered by the trees until you reach the grassy Quay. Here, there are benches from which you can view the little islands and the causeways along the Baltimore coast.

Originally, the present 20 acres of garden was a farm belonging to Fiernan O'Driscoll, until a family named Becher acquired the property of Creagh. The family at one time owned most of this part of western Cork, including Cape Clear, Sherkin, and Mount Gabriel. The daughter of the house, Mary Becher, became the heiress because of a tragic accident in which her father shot her brother. Mary went on to marry into the Wrixons of Ballygiblin, who were a prominent Cork family famous for their hunting exploits. The Wrixon-Bechers, as they then became known, started building the Regency house, with its wide eaves and deep semicircular bow, possibly as a hunting lodge. In 1819, their son William Wrixon-Becher, M.P., married the famous Irish actress, the classical beauty Eliza O'Neil, in the church at Kilfane, County Kilkenny. It was Eliza who designed the serpentine pond and built the octagonal gothic Folly between the pond and the sea.

This now-ruined building is soon to be restored. From what you can make out, it must have had a downstairs room with a fireplace, perhaps in which to take tea and shelter from a squall, and then a staircase leads to the roof, where, on a clear day, there is a splendid watchtower's view of the estuary.

The pond next to the Folly is edged with green ferns, skunk cabbages (*Lysichiton americanus*), New Zealand flax (*Phormium tenax*), and Tasmanian tree ferns (*Dicksonia antarctica*), as well as more giant Chilean rhubarb, irises, primroses, weeping willows, and bluebells. The moss-covered bark of sycamore and oaks is covered with ferns, and clumps of arum lilies (*Zantedeschia aethiopica*) have their roots deep in the pond bed so they appear to be growing on the water. The soil is acidic, which suits the late-summer hydrangea, with its electric-blue flowers, and in the spring camellias abound.

Walking back up to the house, you pass a giant *Magnolia campbellii*, and suddenly a waft of vanilla warns you that you are approaching the *Azara microphylla* 'Variegata,' which originated in William Gumbleton's magnificent garden at Belgrove, near Cobh, in the nineteenth century. On the lawn to the left of the front of the house is a small thatched summerhouse, in which the Harold-Barrys used to play bridge. Peter called it his Baluba Folly, named for the fierce Baluba tribe in the Congo. He felt that it increased the Rousseaulike "clearing in the jungle" impression. Next to the summerhouse is an unusual Australian shrub not often seen in Irish gardens, the Braidwood waratah (*Telopea mongaensis*), which has bright red flowers in late spring.

Through camellia and pittosporum glades, and passing the *Rhododendron* 'Tally Ho,' you come to the walled organic Kitchen Garden, currently undergoing restoration. Here are three series of restored greenhouses for ornamental and propagation purposes. The ornamental one has a flourishing lemon tree, with its delicious scent, and angels' trumpets (*Datura*

Top: After wintering in the greenhouse, the aptly named angel's trumpet produces large yellow flowers in midsummer.

Above: Midsummer is also the time when these decorative ornamental gourds appear in the walled garden.

Above: The peat-stained water of the pond acts like a mirror, reflecting the interlaced branches of the trees.

Brugmansia aurea), flowering quince, *Acacia longifolia*, Cape leadwort (*Plumbago auriculata*), jasmine, and a banana passion fruit (*Passiflora mollissima*) that actually produces tasty yellow bananalike fruits. A belt of tall beech trees shelters the garden. A Czechoslovakian-style log hen house is home to a variety of exotic fowl, such as Silkies, Morans, Plymouth Rocks, bronze turkeys, and guinea fowl, all of which scratch around, making dust beds in what was the old orchard. Sorrel, leeks, broad beans, sprouting broccoli, globe artichokes, rhubarb, chives, mint, and borage grow in boxwood-edged beds. There are edgings of wild strawberries and rows of raspberries. A cottage garden area at one end has clematis scrambling over wooden arches and a variety of flowering herbaceous plants with lots of different herbs, as well as comfrey.

In spring, the avenue in front of the house is filled with the scarlet flowers of the towering Chilean firebush next to tree-sized rhododendrons. Indian mallows (*Abutilon*), tree peonies, mimosa, which flowers in midwinter, and lots of magnolias flourish in the mild climate. The grass verges are left to grow wild, with flowers such as bluebells, buttercups, scabious, cowslips, and orchids. A south-facing perennial bed against a thick yew hedge has been planted to screen the parking lot. There is much wildlife in the gardens.

Herons frequently examine the pond for delicacies, and there are pheasants and partridges, barn owls, and the little ring-necked doves that pair for life.

Two friends of Peter Harold-Barry, Kenneth Lambert and Martin Sherry, who cared for him during his last few years, have now lived here since 1991. Martin Sherry had previously worked for the National Trust in England. Kenneth Lambert is a conservator of houses and gardens. The work they undertook was tremendous, not only on the grounds, but also in the house itself. The garden had become very overgrown in the last years of Peter's life, and they spent the first three years clearing and tidying, discovering lost vistas, making good the network of meandering paths, bringing in new topsoil, and cutting back the bamboo. Their determination and efforts have been helped by a team of gardeners from the Great Gardens of Ireland Restoration Programme. FAS, the state employment project, has also been of assistance. Their goal is to save as much of Peter Harold-Barry's beautiful garden and as many of his plants as possible. Their efforts in retaining the atmosphere of this balmy and aromatic place will surely encourage the summer visitors who flock to the sailing center of nearby Baltimore to turn their rope-soled shoes toward exploring such a gentlemanly jungle.

Above: The lush planting around the pond, devised by Peter Harold-Barry in imitation of a jungle scene painted by the French artist Douanier Rousseau. The house seems to stand in a sunlit clearing.

Plan of Creagh

1. Wood
2. Fern Walk
3. Malachy's Field
4. Boat House and Slip
5. Sir John's Walk
6. Quay
7. The Cache
8. Mill Pond
9. Old Mill Folly
10. Hen Hilton House
11. Kitchen Garden
12. Baluba Hut
13. Jungle Walk
14. Garden Entrance

DERREEN
COUNTY KERRY

Derreen stands as testimony to the extreme determination and foresight of one man, the fifth Marquis of Lansdowne (1845–1927), who inherited the demesne as a very young man in 1866. The gardens lie on a bare rocky promontory in the Bay of Kilmakilloge in the Barony of Glanerought, near Kenmare in County Kerry. Though protected from the worst of the elements by the mountain of Knockatee at their rear and, on the other side of the bay, by a majestic-looking range of barren hills that stretches down the Beara Peninsula, it is amazing that these gardens were ever planted at all, given that their rocky wilderness location offered little top soil or shelter. The fourth Marquis of Lansdowne had initiated the planting of the area in 1863, but it was the fifth Marquis who really became fascinated by Derreen and began planting in 1870. He understood the potential of the soft Kerry climate, which suffers few frosts and has 80 inches of rainfall a year.

Previous page, main picture: Antique rhododendrons drop scarlet petals on soft peaty soil in a scene repeated throughout the mild southwest of Ireland.

Previous page, detail: Where rhododendrons flourish, camellias will also thrive.

Above: A pirate's dream hideaway island, now linked to the mainland by a rickety bridge, is a part of the garden.

In addition, the fifth Marquis took advantage of the amazing array of plants and seeds that this country's intrepid explorers and professional plant-hunters were bringing to Ireland from all over the world. It was as if the deep mountain gorges of China, the rain forests of South America, the uplands of New Zealand, and the native pine trees of British Columbia were all tipped into this pocket of profuse growth in an otherwise bare landscape in the west of Ireland. Dr. Augustine Henry from County Londonderry had opened the treasure chest of China's wild flora while he served there as a customs official.

The fifth Marquis stayed at Derreen with his wife for three months of every year from 1870 to the 1920s, except in 1883 and 1894, when he was only able to snatch a few weeks between his postings, first to Canada as Governor General and then to India as Viceroy. Over the years, the gardens took shape following his carefully laid-out plans.

The original scrub of holly and brambles that covered the land was replaced with European black pines (*Pinus nigra*) and Monterey pines (*P. radiata*), as well as groups of griselinia, which are now 35 feet high. Along the shore line a belt of holm oak (*Quercus ilex*) and groups of the New Zealand flax (*Phormium tenax*), interspersed with *Olearia albida* and *Pittosporum tenuifolium*, were planted to shelter the rest of the gardens from the sea. Then the topsoil was brought in. The huge drainage system, which crisscrosses the garden, was installed, providing essential drainage for the many rhododendron plants that were introduced in 1875. The fifth Marquis planted 100 *Rhododendron arboreum* hybrids, but before long they had grown to such a size that they were cutting off all light and air from the narrow walks. The decision was made to cut most of them down. Today just a few specimens remain – all well over 60 feet high. In the 1890s, the paths were

Above: The placid waters and rugged mountains of Kilmakilloge Harbour. To create a garden here the first essential is shelter, so pine trees were planted to provide it.

Above: Tree ferns were once imported from New Zealand and Australia into Europe as ships' ballast. However, gardeners soon discovered that they would flourish in sheltered frostfree places. Now they are the quintessence of gardens in Cork and Kerry.

Opposite above: The young fronds of the tree ferns unfurl themselves from perfect fiddle heads. These specimens are probably more than a century old.

Opposite below: A majestic tree fern with its crown of feathery fronds is growing towards the light from the dappled shade of the forest floor.

laid out, the lawns were seeded, and the sessile oaks (*Quercus petraea*) were cleared from around the house. Scots pines (*Pinus sylvestris*), groves of bamboo, tree ferns, and shrubs of all kinds sheltered the lawns. The peat bank from which Lord Lansdowne's tenant drew his household turf had been made into a bog garden, and the existence of the former farmland was only visible in places under the vegetation by the traces of a bank or ditch.

The house itself is swathed in gorgeous creeping vines. From the lawn, directly in front of the house, a smooth mound of rock emerges like a piece of moonstone left behind from the Ice Age. From here the vastness of the mountainous amphitheater in which you are standing becomes apparent. Sheltered by the mountains and dark green conifers are three rhododendrons, two with delicate lemon flowers with a brown center and one with pale pink flowers. In early spring, a carpet of bluebells surrounds an old Monterey pine. A Persian ironwood tree and an Irish yew frame this stunning Himalayan vista. From here to the Boat House, you walk through a forest of rhododendrons and azaleas. In the spring, the path is flanked by a veritable array of color, with pink, red, and blue azaleas and a group of *Rhododendron* 'Fragrantissimum,' whose white blossoms, tinged with pink, release a spicy nutmeg scent. A tall *Pieris formosa*, with lily-of-the-valley-shaped white flowers, stands next to a tree fern (*Dicksonia antarctica*). A *Rhododendron sinograndle* is protected by a large *Chamaecyparis lawsonia* 'Erecta Viridis.'

Leaving the huge-leaved rhododendrons behind, you cross a shaky wooden bridge to arrive at a small island packed with more pine and oak trees. During the eighteenth century, it is said that there was a souterrain on the island used to hide contraband, such as tobacco and brandy, which were smuggled into the bay by French ships. At this time, it seemed that everyone in the area was involved in smuggling, including the tenant of Derreen. "Wool went out and brandy came in; everyone had a share of the profits and all were leagued together to defeat the officials of the government," wrote the nineteenth-century historian J.A. Froude, who often stayed at Derreen and documented much of the local folklore in his book, *The Two Chiefs of Dunboy.*

This treacherous part of the coast has seen many wrecks in its history. In his book, *Glanerought and the Petty-Fitzmaurices,* the sixth Marquis of Lansdowne recounts many stories, among them the fate of a West Indian merchantman, *The Planter.* In 1775, this ship, laden with silver and tea, reached Ballinaskelligs Bay in great distress. The tenant of Derreen at the time was Morty O'Sullivan McFinin Duff, Chief of the O'Sullivan clan. One of his illegitimate sons offered his services to *The Planter* and with great skill brought the half-disabled ship into Kilmackilloge harbor, conveniently close to his father's residence. The ship was promptly ransacked and became a total wreck. In those days, Morty O'Sullivan, with two near relations, controlled the whole of the western end of Glanerought, into which the representatives of the landlord seldom ventured with impunity. Once, when Morty was an old sick man, Lord Shelburne, the prime minister of England at that time and later the first Lord Lansdowne, sent a present of a case of claret. It is said that

Morty dragged himself from his bed onto the big rock in front of the house and, with dreadful imprecations against the donor, solemnly broke every bottle – anything except undiluted spirits was considered an insult by the old chiefs of the clan O'Sullivan.

Looking back toward the house from the island, you can see nothing but a border of trees with the hills beyond. The gardens stay enclosed in a secret world. Turning into the Middle Walk, there stands a *Rhododendron griffithianum*, with its ethereal white flowers lighting up the dark shadows, and another rhododendron with blood-red trumpets. The grove of bamboo and forest of tree ferns are ringed by giant thujas, all of which combine to evoke a scene from a typical Japanese painting: a jungle seen through a gap in the trees, slate-gray sea, pine trees, wooden bridge, and cone-shaped islands.

If you turn left again and take the granite steps up the hill, you enter a green tunnel and arrive into the light at Froude's Seat, under the *Rhododendron* 'Loderi King George.' From here you can look out over the silvery water to the distant hills across the mussel beds. Here, in springtime, a grass path snakes through a mass of bluebells, which can be seen from the house. Conifers are interspersed with slender eucalyptus trees so tall you can't

Above: The moist and mellow climate at Derreen allows moss to cloak not just the tree trunks but also the outcrops of old red sandstone. When trees are toppled in storms, they can still live on, like this ancient Cryptomeria japonica, *'Elegans.'*

lean back far enough to see their tops. The tall, evergreen Tasmanian Huon pine (*Lagarostrobus franklinii*) and Sawara cypress (*Chamaecyparis pisifera* 'Squarrosa') make you shiver in their shade. There are high banks of rock above the tree ferns, and rhododendrons light up the gloom in pale pink, pink, and purple. The granite hill has plants and trees growing along its banks as far as the sea, which arch up to reach the light. Walls of rock are covered in vines like in a Brazilian jungle.

Turn left again into the King's Oozy, where King Edward VII and Queen Alexandra planted two commemorative bamboos in 1903. The area is made up of layer upon layer of leaf mold, and avenues of enormous tree ferns have seeded themselves with their roots in the drainage canals. A fragile young camellia flourishes in the shade of the rustling royal bamboos, and the canopy of overhanging trees is now so high that it lets in enough light for plants to thrive below. *Rhododendron sinogrande, R. delavayi, R. falconeri,* and *R. niveum* are now enormously tall, but the long vistas of clipped Victorian "laurel lawns" that once surrounded them have long since gone.

Take the broad stone steps up from the King's Oozy and pass the biggest known specimen of *Cryptomeria japonica,* 'Elegans.' Although its vertical height once reached 60 feet, since being damaged by a gale it has been supported horizontally 6 feet above its original position on what is known as the Glade Walk. Every tree trunk is deep in moss; the rocks, too, are smothered in moss and liverworts. Moving on, you might breathe a sigh of relief once you have passed the menacing-looking Patagonian cypresses (*Fitzroya cupressoides*), with their overhanging branches. You then reach a little terrace cut into the cliff face. Here, at dusk, you can sit on the Knockatee Seat and watch the granite face of that mountain slowly turning pink as the sun sets. Directly below, the chasm is filled with a single rhododendron, which is covered in masses of rose-colored flowers in spring.

It is said that the fifth Marquis employed 40 people to create the garden. In India, he was ideally positioned to bring back rare species from the East, subscribing to the Himalayan plant-hunting expeditions. He also bought many exotic plants from the famous nursery firm of Veitch and from the Waterer Nurseries at Sunningdale in Berkshire, England. In the true tradition of William Robinson, the naturalization of hardy and exotic plants from other countries was such a success that these original plants have spread into large groups of tree ferns, myrtles, and several species of *Gaultheria*. The Chilean lantern trees (*Crinodendron hookerianum*) and firebushes (*Embothrium coccineum*) do as well here as in their native habitat, as do the tall acacias from Australia. The *Eucalyptus globulus* were planted at Derreen as early as 1870 and are among the largest recorded in cultivation. *Drimys winteri, Clethra alnifolia, Myrtus luma,* and *M. lechleriana,* as well as the tree ferns (*Dicksonia antarctica*) all flourish in this warm climate and mountain setting.

Like Creagh, this is another Robinsonian garden, with the advantage that the plantings are older and cover a larger area. The tree ferns are naturalized and the bamboo rampant, and, although a period of neglect allowed them to run wild, they have been hacked back and the skeletons of mature trees resuscitated. There is a published record of the early plantings in the form of a catalog, and, in some ways, Derreen was a trial ground (like the nearby garden of Rossdohan) for plants from Australia and New Zealand. The astonishingly fast rate of growth of many of the species meant that the fifth Marquis was able to see his treasures mature in his own lifetime.

After a long period of inactivity, the estate was inherited by Viscountess Mersey, the granddaughter of the fifth Marquis. She was an avid gardener, who breathed new life into the gardens. Derreen is now owned by her son and daughter-in-law, Mr. and Mrs. David Bigham, who love the garden with a passion. They have recently opened the gates to the public.

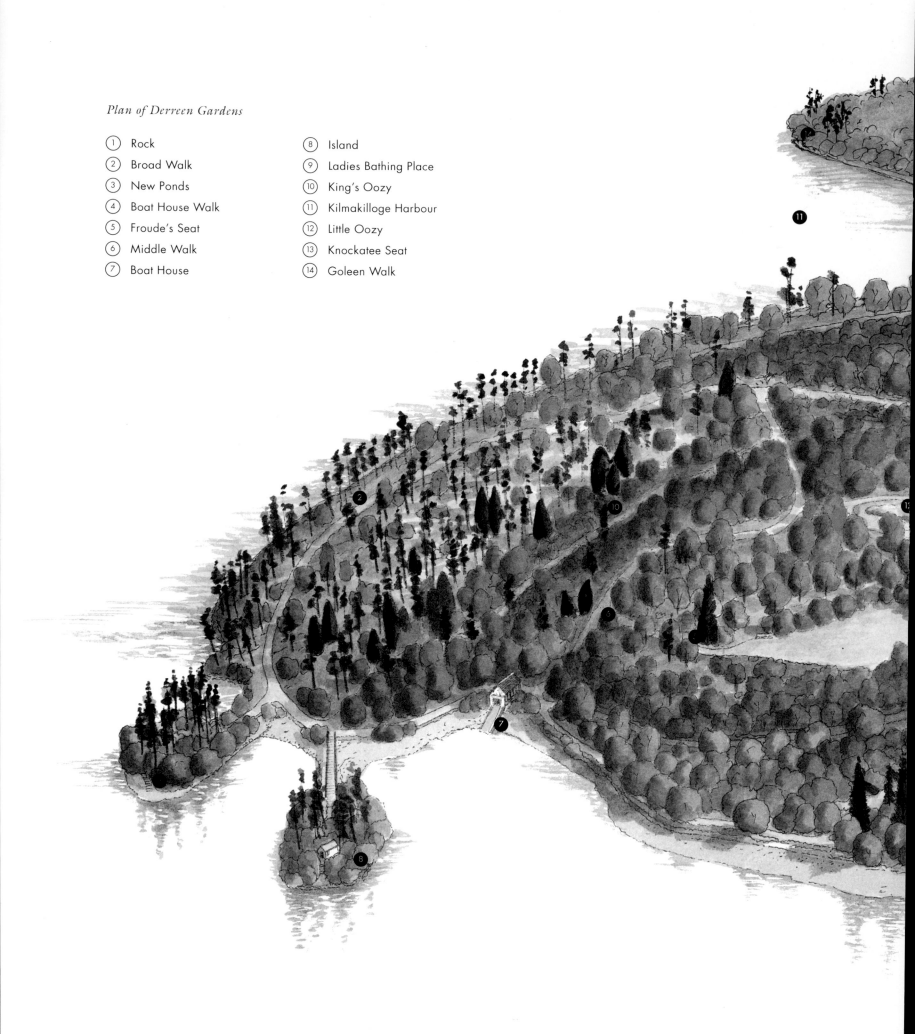

Plan of Derreen Gardens

1. Rock
2. Broad Walk
3. New Ponds
4. Boat House Walk
5. Froude's Seat
6. Middle Walk
7. Boat House

8. Island
9. Ladies Bathing Place
10. King's Oozy
11. Kilmakilloge Harbour
12. Little Oozy
13. Knockatee Seat
14. Goleen Walk

THE DILLON GARDEN
RANELAGH, DUBLIN

Helen Dillon's walled town garden is in the center of Dublin, and yet
tucked away off a main thoroughfare down a shaded dead-end street.
The entrance to her secret world is a simple wooden gate. On the day
of my visit, there had just been a shower, and shafts of sunlight were
streaming onto the front steps of the plain, square eighteenth-century
house. The door was thrown open by a beaming figure with short blonde
hair and blue eyes who wailed in despair, "I can't think why you have
come today – there is nothing to see in the garden at all!"

Helen Dillon's anxiety has not lessened as she has become famous; in
fact, as the reviews of her books, articles, lectures, television appearances,
and garden become increasingly flattering, her artist's desire for perfection,
unachievable in her own eyes, reaches agonizing proportions.

Previous page, main picture: William Robinson said that the California tree poppy (Romneya coulteri) was "the fairest plant that ever came to our land from that country of flowers." It is willful, but very beautiful.

Previous page, detail: Blue delphiniums are one of the attractions of the Dillon Garden.

Above: The informal pavement in the front garden is a foil for foliage and flowers. The large terracotta jar is planted with a trailing raspberry.

Twenty-six years ago, Helen and her husband, Val, walked through the door of 45 Sandford Road and fell in love with the house and what was then an ordinary walled town garden. They have been working on it ever since they moved in, and when they are not toiling in the garden, they can sit in their butter-yellow living room and look out through its long windows at their masterpiece, with its emerald-green lawn and thickly planted beds. It seemed a good omen that Dr. Augustine Henry, the Edwardian plant collector, had lived next door, and that his light orange, faintly spotted *Lilium henryi*, which he brought back from the limestone hills of China, was flourishing at over 7 feet high.

Brought up in the highlands of Scotland, Helen has been a gardener ever since a geranium was given to her when she was a child. She is a voracious plant collector, and Ireland's temperate climate means that she is spoiled in the range of plants she can cultivate. Each year she travels far and wide, bringing back treasures of seeds from the Himalayas, the Alps, New Zealand, South Africa, and South and North America, and propagating them all in her greenhouse. The result is a plant lover's garden containing hundreds of plants in just under one acre of land. Seemingly effortlessly, she brings all the plants together to create a garden that is both attractive and well balanced. Each plant is given the right soil and other growing conditions that would most resemble its natural habitat. She has a crusading desire to encourage American gardeners to try out new plants, and her book, *Garden Artistry,* is written with special reference to American zones of climate as they relate to the plants that she can grow in Ireland.

Helen also has a burning passion for old cultivars. She spends any spare time searching abandoned gardens for old-fashioned plants that need rescuing from obscurity or oblivion, such as the garden forms of the wild double buttercup, hen-and-chickens daisy, and crested ferns. Some of the plants that were grown at the beginning of the twentieth century and died out in mainland Europe and England are still flourishing in her garden. The English National Trust's plant cataloguer was astonished to find the long-vanished double red nasturtium still doing well in Ireland. Helen says these plants have survived because the landscape and gardens of Ireland have not suffered the same changes of use as those in other parts of Europe, and were undamaged by the two world wars.

Helen is particularly attached to plants with Irish connections, and *Viola* 'Irish Molly,' *Agapanthus* 'Lady Moore,' and *Celmisia* 'David Shackleton' (named after her mentor who built up his famous plant collection in another walled garden at Beech Park, County Dublin) have pride of place. Some of her plants have come in direct line from long-departed gardeners of their day, and she feels she has been lucky to have known the tail-end of the last of the great old Irish gardeners. Some of the gardeners she met for lunch would give her gems of plants, with the entreaty that she didn't give them away. Helen's attitude is completely different, and she wants to encourage the whole world to grow these plants.

Nothing has been more influential in encouraging the rising tide of interest in Irish gardens than the publication of Helen's first book, *In an Irish Garden*, which she wrote with the famous designer, the late Sybil Connolly. Her latest book, *Helen Dillon on Gardening*, is a compilation of her weekly gardening columns featured in the *Sunday Tribune*. The columns are as encouraging and instructive as anything by Vita Sackville-West or Anne Scott-James.

To use a garden as a canvas for esthetic effect requires a deep knowledge and love of plants, along with the courage and energy to be prepared to move plants to create the desired overall design. "My fingers are worn to the bone," Helen sighs, "but the garden is never right." She and Val do by far the majority of the work in the garden themselves, prompting sympathetic Americans to send them special soothing hand creams. A robin, in what must now have become a hereditary position, either sits on Val's shoulder or near at hand. Helen's nickname for Val is Grub, and he lives up to his name by taking care of the compost mound. Housed in the brick courtyard at the side of the house where the carriages were kept, the compost emits a delicious smell of freshly mown grass. All the garden material, including dead flowers and shrubs, is shredded and forked into bays with wooden slatted moveable fronts,

Below: The dominant colors in early summer are magenta and purples. The tall grass is a fountain of gold while the modern English rose, 'Graham Stuart Thomas,' contributes a splash of yellow. Standard wisteria, lots of cranesbill, spiky foliage of red-hot pokers and irises, alliums, as well as alpine beds in the gravel, form the structure of the front garden.

Above: Evening light picks out the gold of the ivy around one of a pair of sphinxes that guard the sunken terrace.

where it gradually decomposes and rots down into beautiful friable compost. As you walk down the steps from the house, with the wide green lawn edged by clipped pyramids of box stretching ahead of you, two ivy-trimmed stone sphinxes guard the south-facing terrace. Broad, thickly planted beds on each side of the lawn, inspired by the color combinations at Mount Stewart, County Down, are themselves dissected by almost invisible narrow stone paths. You feel as though you are standing in the middle of the bed itself.

Helen's borders are memorable because she has succeeded in creating a "heavenly muddle." Angel's fishing rods (*Dierama pulcherrimum*) brush your arms as you pass, admiring the cloudy blues and airy mauves in the right-hand bed and hot velvety reds paling to pinks in the left. Everything is flourishing so finely and there are so many faces of flowers, some hanging in bells and

Above: Helen has arranged pots of choice alpines on antique cast-iron tables to provide continual color and interest; they can be protected in the winter.

some in bunches, it is hard to believe that so many plants in such a complex plan could fit into what is such a deceptively simple-looking structure. However, she explains that some plants just can't stand the pace and get squashed to death.

At the end of the green lawn there is a round pond, formal in style, with a fountain, and an arbor in the center of a series of arches which are draped with climbers. There are also apple trees and a Judas tree. Clipped juniper accompanies these while roses and honeysuckle tumble over the arches with foxgloves sheltering underneath them.

If you turn right off the lawn and then pass in between two little sturdy box pillars, you will come up to the greenhouse which is always bursting with delicate, scented, half-hardy plants. A series of garden compartments leads you

*Above: Variegated foliage of euonymus and
ceanothus provide year-round cream and gold,
while the perennials come and go.*

*Opposite: Helen takes every opportunity to
use clipped box in the Yellow Garden. Two dwarf
cones of box are almost smothered
by a mélange of yellow and orange flowers
and green and silver foliage in her recently
planted yellow bed.*

around the edge of the garden walls. The south wall of the house is covered
with climbers, including the sage greens and the powdery grays of the leaves
of *Vitis vinifera* 'Incana' with its edible black grapes. *Bomaria caldesii* is
related to an alstroemeria, and the flowers of the *Ixia viridiflora* from South
Africa look like turquoise-colored tissue paper.

One plant you find here that Helen tells us we will not often find in the
United Kingdom is *Billardiera longiflora* from Tasmania, which has shiny
navy blue berries and pale yellow flowers. There are pansies, and an *Abutilon
megapotamicum* with its red petticoat petals. Pots adorn the terrace, and
pans of alpines stand as decoration on the wrought-iron tables. The white
and pink daisylike stars of *Rhodohypoxis* come from the Drakensburg
mountains in South Africa and will flower for three months, as long as you
remember to water them well throughout the summer and keep them dry in
the winter (to remind them of being covered by mountain snow) in their
terracotta alpine pans.

Walking around the garden, it becomes evident that the story of its
development reflects the story of Helen's life. Many of the plants in the
garden hold precious memories for her, and she refers to them as fondly as she
would to special friends or relatives. She proudly introduces me to the
'Duchesse de Brabant,' a pale apricot tea rose that she was given as a cutting
in a graveyard in Virginia – it is the rose that Teddy Roosevelt always wore in
his buttonhole. A bearded light-blue iris, which is an old cultivar, was given
to her by the great horticulturist Graham Stuart Thomas, and a cousin
brought back from his vacation the rose 'Marie Pavie' that is climbing on the
trellis. We gaze down at what appears to be a piece of mauve ruched
taffeta striped in pink, which she tells me is an old Irish rose that she came

across in a forgotten garden in County Westmeath. She next introduces the only American resident in the garden, *Clematis viticella*, 'Mrs. Betty Corning,' and I feel as though I am actually meeting the lady herself. She admits that the *Michauxia* seed she brought back from Syria was very easy to grow – it now looks like a huge, upside-down passion flower. The *Nectaroscordum siculum* she describes as coming out in "umbrella-mode," with its little harebell-like, dusty pink flower heads sticking out on long thin stalks. The three-foot-high *Clematis integrifolia* is admirably displayed in a stylish metal basket, an idea for a plant support that she got from Mrs. Betty Farquar, who in turn copied it from the Duchess of Devonshire. *Allium cristophii* has thousands and thousands of mauve stars forming a large ball. Alongside these is the rather phallic *Puya alpestris*, whose fat buds, as Helen explains with a chortle, elongate and then erupt into iridescent, shiny green bells.

There are dense mounds in the gravel of the most unusual alpines, and different-colored starry flower heads look up out of the stone troughs.

Alpines greet you as well when you enter the front garden, which has undergone a transformation from being a mass of plants that were difficult to see properly into a much more open and easily accessible space. A paved terrace of silver-gray Donegal flagstones is now surrounded by judiciously chosen, carefully placed plants, and it is pure delight to sit on the stone seat in the calm of the evening sunshine next to the color and the scent.

One of Helen's worries about her garden is that people will feel intimidated by seeing so many plants in such a comparatively small space. It most certainly is a specialist's garden, but that does not stop the rest of us from enjoying its wonders. She is doing her best to demystify gardening. "I want my garden," she says simply, "to make people feel better."

Opposite: Nectaroscordum siculum *comes from the Balkans, and its seedheads are as elegant as its bell-shaped flowers on their long thin stalks.*

Below left: The rare old Begonia *'Hatton Castle' at the edge of the path that winds behind the Red Border.*

Below right: Two reds that complement each other in the Red Border are the darkest red Scabiosa *'Chile Black' next to the startling lobelias.*

GLENVEAGH CASTLE
COUNTY DONEGAL

Glenveagh Castle is a battlemented, cut-stone, Victorian hunting lodge with a tower and a courtyard built overlooking the blue waters of Lough Veagh. It is surrounded by almost tropically luxuriant gardens in the middle of a valley that was formed during several ice ages. The snout of a glacier ground its way through the encircling sheer granite mountains, leaving behind lakes and streams, corries and glens, which now form the wild and savage scenery of a 25,000-acre National Park.

Before the Irish government took over the conservation of the gardens, there was a long-running American connection with Glenveagh. It began in 1861, when its archetypally wicked Irish landlord, John George Adair, married a beautiful, wealthy, young American widow named Cornelia Richie. Her sweetness and good sense prevailed over the local peoples' bitter dislike of her husband, who had been responsible for evicting 46 of his tenants' families during and after the Famine.

*Previous page, main picture: The turret of
Glenveagh Castle seen through a tracery of
mountain ash, a tree that is native in Ireland.
The red berries are usually devoured rapidly
by birds.*

*Previous page, detail: Dahlia 'Matt Armour,'
a variety unique to Glenveagh, named after
a former head gardener.*

*Above: Henry McIlhenny created this formal
"potager" at Glenveagh.*

After his death in 1885, Cornelia continued to live at Glenveagh, until a
few years before her own death in 1921. She introduced deerstalking in the
1890s and spent most of her time entertaining streams of visitors, laying out
the gardens, and planting and improving the rugged terrain around the castle.
During World War I, she allowed Glenveagh to be used as a convalescent
home for Belgian soldiers. After her death, it was occupied in quick succession
by both sides of the Irish Civil War of 1922. A Harvard professor, Arthur
Kingsley Porter, and his wife bought it in 1929. Here he wrote his book, *The
Crosses and Culture of Ireland*, before disappearing in mysterious and tragic
circumstances while on a walk on the island of Inishbofin.

In 1936, another American with links in the locality, Henry McIlhenny,
bought the property. His grandfather had grown up a few miles from
Glenveagh in the small village of Milford, where his father had owned a shop.
After immigrating to Columbus, Georgia, Henry's grandfather settled in
Philadelphia, where he made a large fortune by inventing the first gas meter.

Henry McIlhenny was on the staff of the Philadelphia Museum of Art, and
then, in his retirement, chairman of the Board of Trustees, he was a
connoisseur and collector of paintings and furniture with which he filled the

castle. His hospitality and generosity at Glenveagh was legendary. Between 1947 and 1983, he must have entertained thousands of people in his highland retreat. He had friends all over the world, including members of the establishment and scholars, as well as numerous poets, painters, authors, musicians, actors, dancers, and even movie stars. They enjoyed his company; he was an exceptionally genial host with an extraordinary store of amusing anecdotes and witty gossip. An invitation to Glenveagh was much sought and discussed, and there was nothing he liked better during the 1950s, '60s and '70s than sending the car to the airport to pick up the latest visitor, perhaps Grace Kelly or Greta Garbo, and to bring them to his romantic, lonely castle.

A knowledgeable gardener himself, Henry McIlhenny employed Lanning Roper and Jim Russell to help with the gardens. For 46 years the gardens grew, so that the hedges, flowerbeds, staircases, arches, walls, stone urns, stags, eagles, and pillars framing vistas became countless. Going on a tour of the garden with Henry McIlhenny, as Desmond Guinness remembers, was always rather like being introduced to various guests at a cocktail party. "This plant was given to me by Lady Leitrim, and this very distinguished one here by Rear Admiral Stevenson," and so on.

Above center: The summer display of the Dahlia *'Matt Armour,' which was raised at Glenveagh perhaps 50 years ago and has been a permanent fixture ever since.*

Above: This small lead cherub holding a pear in one hand, a fruit dish in the other, and sitting on top of a stone ball outside the orangery is just one of the many decorative figures in the Walled Garden.

Garden leads into garden at Glenveagh with bemusing variety, each one hidden from the next, and each one either gazing inward and thickly surrounded by shelter, or else preparing you, with a buildup of well-chosen trees and shrubs, for a dramatic outward view of hillside and lake. Desmond Guinness recalls Henry saying: "I just can't STAND earth," giving the offending substance a fierce prod with his stick and instructing his head gardener to see that it was covered with greenery. The vegetable plots in the Walled Garden were all edged with wild strawberries at his special request, and Philippe Jullian designed him an orangery in which he grew exotics and drank coffee after dinner on summer evenings.

Benevolent and well-organized in everything he did, Henry sold the estate in 1975 to the Irish Office of Public Works to create a National Park, now under the care of Dúchas, the Heritage Service of the Department of Arts, Gaeltacht, and the Islands. In 1983 he gave the castle and gardens to the nation. Three years later, the castle was opened to the public – just a few months after Henry died. It is a strange sensation arriving at the gardens today without its charismatic creator, but it is a compliment to his judgment and taste to see how the planting has matured, and such a success has been

made of the gardens by Dúchas. As is inevitable over a period of time, some details have changed, but the overall effect is splendid, and one almost expects Henry McIlhenny to appear, beaming, at the entrance to the courtyard around which he added more battlements to increase the picturesque effect. I think he would be proud and happy if he could see how it all looks today.

Take the road that leads to the castle winding along the blue lake past mountains, yellow gorse, and silver birches, until you arrive at the Eagle Gate and enter the avenue bordered by rhododendron hedges and banks of hydrangeas leading up to the castle. Here you can have tea in the sunny courtyard paved with black and gray marble, where terracotta lemon pots are planted with azaleas, figs, and camellias. Lining the walls are bushes of bay, trimmed by the frothy leaves of lady's mantle (*Alchemilla mollis*).

The gray stone castle sits on the grass terrace above the lake. The grimness of cut stone is softened by banks of fuchsia, clipped and trained to climb and spread up the walls. The weather here is extremely changeable. Wind is a major hazard, with gales raging through the glen. Calm water can quickly become a seething mass of waves and flying spume. Rainfall is plentiful, with roughly 70 inches a year. Due to the influence of the Gulf Stream, the winters

Above: The stark contrast between the wild and the cultivated. On the far side of Lough Veagh, the rocks and the moorland are in their natural state, while on the near side thickly planted pine trees shelter the castle and its gardens, creating an exceptional micro-climate.

Opposite above: Henry McIlhenny was a discerning collector of antique garden ornaments, which are a feature of Glenveagh.

Opposite below: Great Aztec-like flights of steps leading to a viewing platform from which the photograph on this page was taken.

are mild with little frost and only occasional snow. Windbreaks of Scots and Austrian pines, alders, *Rhododendron ponticum* (which has become a pest), escallonias, olearias, and bamboo were all planted early and provide invaluable shelter. The peaty soil is acidic, and trees are hard to grow in places, but palms, tree ferns, mimosas, fragrant rhododendrons, (which usually live in a greenhouse), and a wide variety of tender plants can all flourish outdoors. Peat and farmyard manure are invaluable for improving the soil.

A path leads from a boathouse to the formal Italian Garden on the south side, where a rectangle of grass is enclosed by clipped griselinia hedges lined with busts of Roman emperors on ivy-clad piers, life-sized stone sculptures, and a large seat. It is a soothing green outdoor room, with few flowers, although tall rhododendrons, mostly blue *R. augustinii* and late-flowering white hybrids, shelter within the hedges. In summer, eucryphias make tall pillars of white against the green background. It is heartening to know that the seemingly frail eucryphias can stand up to the gusting winds.

The Pleasure Ground, to the north of the castle, is a broad sweep of lawn that mimics the contours of the lake. It is completely enclosed by shrubs and trees, planted on the edge of the surrounding mountain gorges among streams hidden by ferny fronds. The green tapestry is subtly highlighted by occasional batches of color – the fiery leaves of a Japanese maple or the springtime blooms of primulas whose seed was collected from Yunnan. There

are tree ferns and Chusan palms, and the fall-coloring katsura tree (*Cercidiphylum japonicum*). Several tall tree rhododendrons, including *R. falconeri* and *R. sinograde*, with their very large leaves and pale yellow flowers, were transplanted from nearby Mulroy House in the 1950s. Hoherias, *Drimys winteri*, and eucryphia reach up into the sheltering pines next to grimacing Balinese sculptures and bright green Japanese *Trochodendron aralioides* trees. Different-colored lichen splay along their branches. The snowdrop tree (*Styrax japonica*) has been cleverly planted hanging over the path, so that in the summer months you can look up to see a spangle of white flowers above you against the inky green of the tangled leaves and branches.

On the way to the Italian Terrace, the classic Irish late-summer combination of montbretia, with its cheerful orange sprays and sharp bright green leaves, and hydrangea, with pale blue blossoms, lines the path. In the distance, through the pine trees, you can glimpse a column topped by a stone pineapple, the symbol of hospitality. Past the Himalayan Garden that is filled in spring with *Meconopsis nepalensis* and has a Ganesh seated tranquilly by the pond, and past the Belgian Walk, built by convalescing Belgians and shaded by a group of *Eucryphia moorei*, you then reach the Italian Terrace, which was designed by Lanning Roper in 1965 with statues and herms chosen by the owner. It is surrounded by rhododendrons and azaleas and has a *Metrosideros umbellata*, which is a mass of red spikes in midsummer. A marble seat offers the opportunity for a welcome rest, surrounded by the humming of bees.

After you have walked on a short way, the calm that has been distilled from these shady groves of plants and trees is suddenly shattered as you go through yet another exotic urn-topped gate into the riot of color and activity in the French-style *jardin potager* inside the Walled Garden. Nothing is hidden from view and a swath of old-fashioned red dahlias cuts across one end in front of the elegant Gothic Conservatory. Vegetable and fruit trees are planted in neat rows between hedges, with spirals of clipped boxwood at each end. There is a brick terrace and standard bay trees in pots. Apple trees, fruit bushes, sweet peas, roses, artichokes, beetroot, potatoes, beans, peas, borage, and mint are all in beds divided down the middle by two great perennial beds. Each garden gate has a different feature on the top of the posts, and water bubbles from a stone dolphin fountain built into a wall.

Slipping through a gate, you come to a lovely rocky glen with moss-covered rocks and trees. There is a steep flight of 67 steps – dramatic in their austere, almost Aztec simplicity – which, if not leading to a heart attack, certainly nowhere else, because at the top all that is waiting is the most incredibly beautiful view of the castle, lake, and mountainside. In spring, the steps are surrounded by a huge mass of white flushed with pink, heavily scented *Rhododendron ciliatum*, which seeds freely in the moss.

Throughout the the garden there are different views across the landscape, all carefully hidden by hedges and planted areas until the last minute. Coming across a seat in a clearing from which you can enjoy wild panoramas of breathtaking natural beauty is one of the abiding joys of this garden.

Above: Close-up of the fountain showing the dolphin base.

Opposite above: An ornamental dolphin fountain is surrounded by vases in the potager.

Opposite below: Young apple trees under-planted with pink mallows to provide color in the upper section of the potager – in the distance are the white flowers of eucryphia.

Plan of Glenveagh Castle

1. Boat House
2. Italian Garden
3. Swiss Walk
4. View Garden
5. Rose Garden
6. Walled Garden
7. 67 Steps
8. Viewing Terrace
9. Belgian Walk
10. Himalayan Garden
11. Italian Terrace
12. Pleasure Ground
13. Lough Veagh

GLIN CASTLE
COUNTY LIMERICK

The gardens at Glin Castle are in a continuous state of rediscovery and re-creation, and there is always something to learn about their history and horticulture. Precariously balanced on the banks of the River Shannon as it roars toward its tidal estuary, the castle itself stands braced to withstand the full onslaught of the Atlantic weather, thereby protecting the gardens that flow gently up the hill behind it. Viewed from a boat on the water, the castle presents a fairy-tale façade as it nestles among high trees between blue bands of water and sky. Its setting in the landscape is highly dramatic, and the more I live here, the more I wonder at the subtlety and good sense of the original builders. A network of box-drains, lined and edged with stone, some at an extraordinary depth of 13 feet, crisscross the gardens, guiding turbulent springs away from the house and keeping the gardens as dry as possible. In early February, the field that runs down to the river in front of the house is glassy with water from the rising high leap-tides.

Previous page, main picture: Lupines, clipped box, and golden Irish yews frame the rustic temple used as shelter from the gentle spring rain. Made from wood thinnings and strategically placed rope, it is built into the stone wall as the focus for the path that divides the upper end of the walled garden.

Previous page, detail: The rose called "Narrow Water" has never flowered better than since its move from the Walled Garden to a new position by the edge of the stream in the Pleasure Grounds.

Above: A ring of mock standing stones situated high on a bank behind the Pleasure Grounds. From here there is a heady view between the trees to the River Shannon below.

The first Norman FitzGerald castle in Limerick, Shanid, built in 1197, is now a ruined fragment of a keep on a motte high above the pasture lands of West Limerick, about eight miles from Glin. "Shanid-Abu," meaning "Shanid forever," was the Geraldine war cry, and the words decorate the plaster ceilings in the present Glin Castle. The first recorded entry for the Knight of Glin is in documents dated 1425. Some time before then, the Geraldines built a castle on the little river that runs into the Shannon, where they lived speaking Gaelic, marrying daughters of neighboring chieftains, and leading a feudal life. They owned many of the castles between Glin and Limerick and many thousands of acres of land. In 1600, this castle in Glin was besieged and razed to the ground by Queen Elizabeth's general, Sir George Carew, leaving only the stone stump with a gaping empty window that you see on driving into the village today. After this calamity the Geraldines lived in hiding in fear of their lives, until they moved to the place where I live today. They built the long, low, thatched house one room thick, which eventually evolved into the two-storied wing of today's Glin Castle.

Colonel John Batemen FitzGerald, the twenty-fourth Knight of Glin, began building the main part of the castle – a plain, bow-windowed Georgian house – in about 1780. His English wife, Margaretta Maria Fraunceis Gwyn, took particular interest in the delicate plasterwork of the hall, from harps and vines to the garlands of flowers and sheaves of wheat that decorate the ceiling. There are plasterwork dolphins that reflect the real-life ones to be seen in the river, and over the Venetian window looking out into the garden from the

flying staircase float white plasterwork cornucopias. There must have been a garden of sorts when the house was built, but it appears that military matters were the main concern of the twenty-fourth Knight of Glin. Margaretta and the Knight's only son, John Fraunceis FitzGerald, was only 12 when his father died in 1803, so he went to his grandparents' house to be brought up at Forde Abbey in Dorset, England, where there were extensive gardens.

On graduating from Cambridge, John Fraunceis returned to Glin and was determined to embellish his demesne in a manner befitting his family's romantic past. He castellated the house and stable yard with pastrycook battlements, built gimcrack Gothic lodges at each gate, a tiny white castellated eye-catcher (the bathing lodge) on the edge of the river, the high stone-walled Kitchen Garden, and the Hermitage on the hill behind the Pleasure Grounds. He brought over a gardener from Somerset, one William Bicknell, in 1822 to lay out the tree planting, and the bones of the garden were put in place. In place of the old road that cut through the demesne, he arranged for the engineer Alexander Nimmo to build a new road and sea wall. This imposing road, cleverly hidden from view by a new hidden ditch constructed to hold back the front field, now snaked along the coast. Travelers from Foynes to Tarbert now had a much easier journey, as they were saved the climb up the hill through the middle of the knight's demesne. Today, peering out of the dining-room windows, you will sometimes see the oddly disconnected top of a passing school bus apparently floating unaided along the top of the ditch.

Above: The remains of a Victorian garden with tree ferns and bamboos lead up to this forgotten early nineteenth-century Hermitage that was once hidden by brambles. It now stands in a glade surrounded by young oak trees.

Above: A formal garden room without walls tempts you out of the castle onto the terrace that is trimmed with huge balls and standard domes of clipped bay. The yellow Banksian rose clambers around the crenellations, and all is sheltered by a Monterey pine.

The entrance to the property took the visitor through the new Gothic lodge in the village, in which the "Knight of the Women" or "*ridire na mBan*" as John Fraunceis became known locally, installed his mistress. Entering a long avenue of trees, a thick band of woodland cut the sight of the water until you rounded a corner. Emerging out of the green gloom into the light again, the impact of the view before you was, as it is now, breathtaking. A huge green field slopes down toward the wide, sparkling river with the white bathing lodge outlined against it, and the whole of County Clare seems to be laid out in front of you on the other side of the water.

Not much has changed since those days, except that great stands of Chilean rhubarb line the road before you reach this view, and Tom Wall, the gardener, has taken the place of the mistress in the lodge. After the Famine and during Victorian times, nothing very much happened and the family lived frugally with no extra cash to expand or change the buildings or the garden. The "Cracked Knight" (John Francis Eyre FitzGerald, son of the "Knight of

the Women") rode his horse up the front stairs, and his son the "Big Knight" downed a bottle of whiskey a day while his sensible wife steered the estate safely through the Land Wars.

In 1892, the garden sprang to life again with the marriage of my husband's grandfather to Lady Rachel Wyndham Quin. Sensitive and artistic, she planted the hill behind the house with thousands of daffodil bulbs given to her by her friends, the Dorrien Smiths of Tresco on the Isles of Scilly. She planted the specimen conifers, the Chilean lantern bush (*Crinodendron hookerianum*), the monumental red cedars (*Thuja plicata*), the *Drimys winteri*, and the now-massive *Pinus radiata* beside the castle. Had she lived longer, the garden would certainly have flourished. Yet, sadly, she was to die young, soon after my father-in-law's birth, and a cloak of sadness fell over the whole demesne. My husband's grandfather had a stroke in 1910, which left him in a wheelchair, and life was pretty miserable until my mother-in-law, Veronica Milner, came here as a girl of 18 in 1929.

Above top: Pink and white cosmos mean mid-summer in the walled garden.

Above: Lupines have always been grown at the foot of the greenhouse steps.

Veronica immediately set about brightening up the whole place. Clearing away the laurels and brambles that were growing up to the windows and executing the pampas grass on the lawn, she recast the formal paths and planted all the lovely magnolias, cherries, and dogwoods that flutter and glimmer in spring along the sides of the lawns. The sprawling Himalayan dogwood is covered in white blossoms in spring and produces strawberrylike fruit in summer. The sundial in the middle of the lawn is surrounded by a yew hedge, and she built the low, swooping wall that divides the garden from the daffodil hill, centering it with a graceful Persian ironwood tree (*Parrotia persica*). Veronica also planted the simple green rectangle of hedge with curving ends outside the drawing-room windows and planted snowdrops in circles around all the trees. In her day, the castle was white-washed every summer by two men suspended in baskets, swinging somewhat precariously from the battlements.

On the garden side of the castle, she laid down a terrace of Liscannor flag iris and planted two standard pompoms of bay, which have now become two great bell-shaped domes. Her yellow Banksian rose twines around the smoking-room window. In spring, the ground around the oak tree on the hill is covered with bluebells. Pale-colored rhododendrons line the path to the stream. Also in spring, the kowhai from New Zealand stands in a pool of saffron-colored pollen across the path from the tall *Magnolia campbellii*, with its wine glass-shaped pink petals that are blown all over the lawn in March. Veronica took cuttings of the camellia trees at nearby Tarbert House which quickly grew into abundant shrubs bearing stiff, scarlet flowers with pointed petals, and have flowered profusely ever since. A side avenue of cordylines leads to a white embroidered wrought-iron gate in the garden wall.

During World War II, my mother-in-law sold the produce of the Kitchen Garden at the infant Shannon Airport at nearby Foynes. Seaplanes landed here with their glamorous passengers, including European kings and queens, diplomats, American generals, spies, and movie stars. All the passengers needed to be fed and were often brought home to Glin to stay.

My mother-in-law came from both a gardening and an artistic background. Her mother left us a collection of watercolors from the 1930s of the walled Kitchen Garden as it was then, with a splendid perennial bed and the highest eucalypts in Ireland (which have since blown down) towering over the garden wall. After my father-in-law's untimely death from tuberculosis, my mother-in-law kept the whole estate going. Six years later, in 1953, she married Ray Milner and together they restored the castle.

I have had a dilemma since coming to live here. On one hand, I have not wanted to spoil what is here or detract from its feeling of enclosed antiquity. On the other hand, we have also been infected by the most virulent attack of the "improvements" virus. Tom has built a rustic temple in the Kitchen Garden to protect a marble statue of a headless Andromeda chained to her rock. The hens live in a Gothic henhouse, and pears, fig trees, and clematis now line the noble gray stone walls. In the greenhouse, small black grapes flourish from vine cuttings given to my mother-in-law by Dick Charteris from Cahir Park, County Tipperary. A fuchsia hedge trims the orchard, and a lovely semicircular garden seat was given to us by the nuns when they left their convent near Mount Trenchard. The bees take offense only if one stands directly in their flight path in front of one of the hives.

The small Gothic Hermitage slowly resurfaced after much digging and drying out until a pebble floor was revealed under a brick-vaulted coved ceiling. Ferns, Solomon's seal, and oak trees have been planted all around, with clouds of windflowers that are followed by primroses. The Woodland Walk has been created, its beginning marked by a wave of wild garlic. Across the stream, you turn up a small incline past conifers and specimen trees until you reach a stunning view over the steel ribbon of the Shannon. Shrubs have been planted to see if they can withstand the west winds, and an octagonal thatched Gothic shelter and seat are planned. Every year trees are blown down and much agonizing goes on about what to plant in place of them. "We are very vulnerable to experts here," Tom sighed plaintively a few winters ago, as we argued our way around the Pleasure Grounds wondering whether to plant a maze or a boxwood edging around the castle or have clipped yews marching up the central path. In the end we have done nothing, perhaps because we know that the garden we already have is the most precious of all.

Below: An avenue of clipped yews in their steel corsets divide the walled garden and are seen through a fuchsia tunnel. The comfortable Edwardian garden seat beckons on hot, sunny afternoons.

Plan of Glin Castle

1. Gothic Entrance
2. Woodland Walk
3. Standing Stones
4. Hermitage
5. Kitchen Garden
6. Yew Avenue
7. Edwardian Seat & Pond
8. Rustic Temple
9. Old Farmyard
10. Stables
11. Gothic Lodge
12. River Shannon

ILNACULLIN
COUNTY CORK

Ilnacullin ("Island of the Holly") is the name of a garden, also known as Garinish, or the Italian Garden, that was started in 1910 on an island in a beautiful inlet off Bantry Bay in County Cork. After leaving Killarney, the road dips and weaves past lakes, through tunnels and along the edge of cliffs, until finally you arrive at sea-level in Glengarriff, where you take a ferry to the garden. There are frequent ferries leaving three different jetties, the middle one of which must be the most romantic quay – near a waterfall surrounded by islands just a short distance off the main street of the village. Stepping onto the boat, the outer world seems to recede. Removed from reality, it is as if you are have a part in a play, as the boat chugs out into the middle of the watery theater. Lime-green hills and mountainous peaks act as your auditorium, lakes glint in the folds of rocky precipices, and little ferries crisscross the ocean.

Seals wait languorously, like mermaids, for the tide to rise and float them off their seaweed-draped rocks, and a heron, disdainful and alert at his post, refuses to acknowledge you. You begin to get an idea of what the atmosphere must have been like nearly a hundred years ago, and what it was that prompted the beautiful Violet le Strange to tell her cousin Constance Markievicz that she had to live here. She had recently married John Annan Bryce, M.P., and was sailing past the barren island after she had spent the summer at Glengarriff Castle.

It was such a peculiar idea at the time to suddenly attempt to create a garden on a completely barren island in the middle of the bay. Could it have been just a whim on their part, or was there more to the Bryces' plan to create a microclimate on what has become almost a botanical Noah's Ark? Could it have been the miraculous ecological recolonization of the island of Krakatoa after the stupendous eruption of its volcano in 1883 when it was reduced to a barren lunar landscape? Annan Boyce had spent time in the Far East and was a member of the National Geographic Society and thus would have known all about this event. Or could they have gained inspiration from a visit to the lush plantings of the Borromeo Gardens on Isola Madre, that had once been a bare rocky island in the middle of Lake Como in Italy, surrounded by mountain ranges? Although there is no evidence that either actually visited the gardens on Isola Madre, it is quite possible that they both did. It is a question which specialists who are interested in the garden often debate. Today we can only speculate about what prompted their decision.

In 1910, the island of Ilnacullin belonged to the British War Office.
The only structure here was a Martello Tower which had been built in 1800
in the anticipation of fending off an invasion by Napoleon. The Bryces bought
the island, tower and all. They soon realized that their prize would be
continually buffeted and swept by Atlantic gales, and they began the task
of blasting the rock and bringing over topsoil and humus from the mainland
to boost the existing thin, shallow, and peaty soil. The fundamentals of
establishing shelter were well understood in Ireland at that time, and the
Royal Dublin Society awarded premiums for the planting of shelter belts.
A thick coniferous fringe around the outer edge of the island was soon in
place to ward off storms.

The Bryces commissioned Harold Peto, the eminent English architect-
turned-landscape designer known for his work at Iford Manor in Wiltshire
and in the south of France, to build their mansion and lay out the garden.
Harold had a great love of Italy. Perhaps, looking out over Bantry Bay, he was
reminded of the Bay of Naples or even Vesuvius. Maybe he was inspired by
the paintings of Veronese (1528–1588), in which the landscape is seen almost
through a frame. It is possible that the inspiration for the Ionic order for the

Above: Temple of the Winds, a viewing terrace from which you can see across the water to the old, bare, heather-covered, sandstone peaks of the Caha Mountains.

Opposite: The island of Ilnacullin lies snugly in the shelter of the hills of Cork and Kerry.

Above: The clock tower at the corner of the Walled Garden is all that is visible on Ilnacullin when one looks down from the Martello Tower. The pine trees and cypresses provide the essential shelter belt for the hidden garden.

Opposite above: There are many different varieties of angel's trumpets – this one with red and yellow flowers blooms in the late summer at Ilnacullin.

Opposite below: The entrance to the Walled Garden, framed by an large-leaved, evergreen magnolia and a fuchsia in full bloom.

capitols and the use of different-colored marbles for the pillars came from the Villa Giulia in Rome. Indeed, the enclosed and sunken gardens in the remains of Pompeii and Herculaneum would have been noble precedents for the garden at Illnaculin.

In spite of Edith Wharton's warning in *Italian Villas and Their Gardens*, published in 1904, that "a marble sarcophagus and 12 twisted columns will not make an Italian garden," Annan Bryce accepted Peto's architectural plans, although he did not like his horticultural ones. Being a plantsman himself, Annan took over the planning and gathering of the plants, so that patron and architect worked harmoniously together. They employed 100 men for three years before the outbreak of World War I. The vast mansion of five stories to have been built near the Martello Tower was never completed. Instead, the gardener's cottage was enlarged, and it was here that the artist Æ (George Russell) and the author and playwright George Bernard Shaw would sometimes come and stay. It was also here that the legendary Scottish head gardener, Murdo Mackenzie, eventually lived.

Four years after the death of Annan Bryce in 1924, Murdo came to look after the garden with Annan's widow, Violet, and her son, Rowland. The garden that we see today is largely the work of this genial and knowledgeable Scot. After his retirement 50 years later, he would take people around the island bearing a marvelous Scottish weeding tool as a walking stick with which he rooted out any weeds that caught his eye. These weeds included millions of seedlings of *Griselinia littoralis,* planted for shelter in bygone days. One day, Murdo spotted a variegated leaf among all the green ones. He carefully cut away all the green shoots, leaving the variegated one, which slowly asserted itself. This original plant is now a tree, and *Griselinia littoralis* 'Bantry Bay' with its pale yellow-and-green leaves is a tender plant to be cherished.

The initial Italianate ideas for the planting were not very successful. The Bryces quickly understood that the landscape had to be invented first in order to create a mellow microclimate, and to complete the envisioned planting schemes, they needed to gather plants from all four corners of the earth. The result is a layout in which a disciplined compartmented architectural framework, whose walls provide support against which the shrubs can be trained and supported, is combined with glorious sweeps of wild untrammeled Robinsonian plantings.

The view of the lily pond and steps leading up to the pavilions of the Italian Garden is well known, with wisteria twining around the honey-colored Bath stone loggia and dwarf bonsai in pots. The crumpled larch is said to be 300 years old. There is a drowsy aura on the flagstone terrace and it gets intensely hot in summer. Because of the moisture and humidity, everything grows faster than in other parts of Ireland, which gives the impression that the plants and trees on the island are much more mature than they really are.

The raised beds around the terrace are filled with treasures such as Australian bottlebrushes, including the crimson *Callistemon salignus* 'Murdo Mackenzie,' several different Indian mallows, including *Abutilon* 'Ashford Red' and 'Cloth of Gold,' and the enchanting tiny-leaved netting plant *Corokia* hung with the deep purple- and blue-flowered *Clematis* x *durandii,* a hybrid from France that has no tendrils and therefore needs support. The New Zealand tea trees (*Leptospermum*) are splashed with pink or white flowers in late spring and early summer, and have to be protected by wooden frames and sacking during frosty winter nights. The dwarf tea trees called 'Kiwi' are planted in pots and the crushed leaves smell delicious, and there is also a very rare tea tree with bicolored petals of pink and white called 'Rowland Bryce,' which was given to the owner of Treseders Nursery in Cornwall by Murdo, and introduced by them in the early 1970s. Among many others that would usually live indoors, the delicate white, scented *Rhododendron* 'Lady Alice Fitzwilliam' lives happily on the terrace all year round. The unusual *Pseudowintera colorata,* which rarely grows to more than three feet, has already reached 23 feet, but this seems quite mundane compared with the shining greenery of its relative, *Drimys winteri.* Just breathing the air in this enclosure makes you feel that you are in a magically charged atmosphere.

The craggy bastions that rise up from the hillsides are smothered with rambling roses, carefully trained and pinned across the face of the rocks. Walking along the path that leads through the trees and shrubs, you emerge at the Happy Valley with its roofless Greek temple at one end overlooking the water, and the Martello Tower at the other, joined together by great swaths of planting on both sides of the *tapis vert* that stretches between them. This

glade surely embodies the paradise garden as described by William Robinson, in which a whole range of exotic plants from all over the world are brought together and planted to make it seem as if they had all occurred naturally. An avenue of Italian cypresses leads to the temple, and then along the sides of the glade are dawn redwoods (*Metasequoia glyptostroboides*), gum trees, the Huon pine (*Lagarostrobue*) from Tasmania, and the native silver birch. The yellow-flowered *Rhododendron macabeaum* from India is a giant compared with the Japanese species *Rhododendron yakushimanum*, whose young growth is wrapped in delicate felt covering in winter. Trees from the Southern Hemisphere, such as the Kauri pine (*Agathis australis*) from New Zealand and the blazing Chilean firebush (*Embothrium coccineum*), mingle with various northern shrubs such as azaleas, dogwoods, and lily-of-the-valley bushes (*Pieris*), as well as other southerners, such as daisy bushes, eucryphia, and mimosa.

Passing by the Bog Garden, where the pickerel weed with a long stalk and blue flower is growing out from under the water, and walking up the steps toward the Martello Tower, you come to the Viewing Point, which looks across the bay to other islands over the mussel beds and lobster pots. Your ears are filled with the sound of the sea. On the downward path, there is a huge tree that was blown down in the storm of Christmas 1998, when a whirlwind swept through the shelter belts and destroyed 64 trees. A giant

Opposite: The Pavilion is a shady place, curtained by wisteria. Its cream Portland stone came from England.

Below: The cool pillared loggia of the Pavilion, offers shelter from the weather in this island garden and was the centerpiece in Harold Peto's garden plan.

Above: Harold Peto's splendid Pavilion is the centerpiece of the garden at Ilnacullin. The main house that he planned was never built. The Pavilion is wreathed with wisteria, and there is a border of phlox beneath the balustrades.

Monterey pine crashed in the storm and can be seen next to the path with its enormous root system laced across the bare rock and clinging to the shallow sandy soil around the edges.

You can seek refuge from the windy hill in the sheltered Walled Garden. Its gray stone pedimented gate has jasmine which climbs through the ironwork of the fanlight. Through the gate and the jasmine you can see beyond to the soft, lush perennial beds that stretch the whole length of the middle of the garden, bringing back memories of those long golden summer afternoons between the two World Wars. The stone walls are dripping with clematis, wisteria, and grapevines, while hydrangeas, lilies, hoherias, apple trees, cherries, magnolias, roses, and camellias are all in a beautiful tangle in the different sections, and the *Michelia doltsopa*, a white-blossomed cousin of the magnolias from the Himalayas and China, grows against a wall next to a marble Roman sarcophagus. There is also an attractive little summerhouse with a pointed roof at one corner and a clocktower at another. You emerge

onto a gravel terrace and a green lawn that was once the lawn-tennis court with the wisteria-clad loggia ahead of you.

Everywhere there are miraculous things growing, the America bull bay (*Magnolia grandiflora*) and *M. delavayi* from China, *Viburnum tomentosum* in elegant layers, a blue cedar of Lebanon, mixed fuchsias in a variety of colors, yuccas, myrtles, and hoherias in late summer. In late spring, there is the wisteria on the stone loggia with *Phlox paniculata* beneath, and in early summer there are the Livingstone daisies scrambling across the rocks.

Nothing goes to waste on the island at Ilnacullin. Compost is made to enrich the soil using seaweed, light prunings, leaves, and grass chippings. The planting is ongoing in the mature gardens. However, because the conditions are constantly changing behind the shelter belts, the garden is continually being redesigned, as though by the very plants and trees themselves. Before 1910, Ilnacullin was simply a bare and rocky island. Now it is often compared with the Garden of Eden.

KILFANE GLEN AND WATERFALL
COUNTY KILKENNY

The story of how the garden at the Kilfane Waterfall was lost, re-discovered, and then carefully restored by Susan and Nicholas Mosse would easily fill several chapters of a novel. When the Mosses first came to live in the Kilfane Dower House in the 1980s, the garden was surrounded by impenetrable woods of *Rhododendron ponticum* and laurel. Ever since, they have worked unceasingly to cut back the encroaching jungle, and the garden that has emerged is a fascinating juxtaposition of two distinct parts.

At first glance, the upper section of the garden seems to fit into a fairly conventional layout of different compartments around the small red Dower House that was once part of the Kilfane demesne. Roses and jasmine climb up a stone barn. The lawn at the back of the house is home to a spreading oak. Mature trees, the stone pond and pergola, and trimmed-back laurel hedges, which had been part of a Victorian garden, have been rescued from the invading forest.

Perennial beds and a beautiful white garden, the Moon Garden, have been planted in the compartments. At the front of the house, a vista has been cut through the surrounding woods showing the distant hill of *Slieve na mBan* and a glade planted with ornamental grasses. The glade leads to William Pye's smoothly flowing fountain, where the water runs down a goblet-shaped funnel within a bronze drum. It is then that you realize that this section of the garden is not a mere re-creation of a Victorian garden in the style of Sissinghurst, but a cleverly laid-out sculpture garden. Modern sculptures, each one made for a particular site, confront and surprise you at each and every turn.

The second part of this garden story is the romantic tale of the rediscovery and restoration of a ruined *cottage ornée*, once a popular feature of eighteenth-century gardens. Discovered deep in a woodland glen at the foot of an artificial waterfall on a tributary of the River Nore, the Mosses have not only restored the cottage to its former glory, but have also created a beautiful woodland garden around it.

The entrance to Kilfane Waterfall Garden is marked by a frog-inhabited pond edged with arum lilies, iris, and the giant Tibetan cowslip (*Primula florindae*). Through dappled birch and oak woods, carpeted with shuttlecock ferns and mosses, a little bridle path takes you to the old orchard, passing the mysterious sculptures that appear to be growing out of the trees. Dry-stone

walls enclose two sides of the orchard, and a hedge of white *Rosa rugosa* runs its length. Circles of crab apple trees are planted in the grass facing a border, which in spring is swept by drifts of indigo grape hyacinths, and in summer is filled with blue-flowered delphiniums, campanulas, and lobelias.

The square pool in the next compartment is edged with granite taken from the old Kilkenny railroad platform. Water lilies and golden orfes inhabit the pool. Stone troughs are filled with Vatican sage (*Salvia sclarea turkestanica*), and a wooden pergola is loaded with clematis and two white roses, 'The Garland' and *Rosa mulliganii*. The latter has an interesting Irish provenance – it is named after the late Dr. Brian Mulligan, the Belfast-born horticulturist who became Director of the University of Washington Arboretum in Seattle.

Next you walk down into the white Moon Garden, entirely enclosed within laurel hedges. Here there are white flowers, such as cosmos, delphiniums, daisies, campanulas, arum lilies, roses, clematis, and mock orange, complemented by the rivers of the silver-leaved lamb's lugs (*Stachys byzantina*) and crisp green boxwood obelisks. The long, narrow laurel-hedged Victorian fern path comes to an end in a wooden-framed, full-length concave mirror that elegantly distorts the image, while reflecting the long green hedges that seem to stretch on to infinity along several avenues behind you.

Another winding path leads temptingly downward, through holly and ivy,

and toward the sound of rushing water. The woodland clearings are thickly planted with yellow columbines, Solomon's seal (*Polygonatum*), ferns, hardy geraniums, dicentras, and foxgloves. As you descend still farther, the path turns sharply, and you can see the valley filled with towering trees. Finally, a rustic stone bridge crosses the river, and, from here, steps lead up through the woodland, past gnarled roots, mossy tree trunks, and arching sprays of laurel. The tops of the sweet chestnuts are just visible on the other bank of the river through the laurel-hung path.

Then, quite unexpectedly, you come across the overhanging roof of a thatched cottage on a smooth green sward. A spiral staircase leads down to the river, and old roses are enclosed in a crisscross fence. You can have tea sitting on rustic chairs, looking onto a waterfall falling from the cliff on the opposite bank. A single red rose drapes the cottage, and honeysuckle, jasmine, and clematis twine through the trellis. Great boulders are carpeted with mosses and cloaked with plants, and the air seems thin from the lack of oxygen. To reach the waterfall, cross the bridge and follow the steps that wind through the forest back up the hill. Some of the boulders have been made into a seat, where you can sit and gaze across the river at the cottage.

The big house at Kilfane is two miles up the road, and both parts of the present garden were once part of its demesne. The house still stands in the middle of its landscaped park (not open to the public) surrounded by majestic trees. A purple beech, sweet chestnuts, and giant redwoods are part of the plantings, and a Folly opposite the house stands in the middle of a dried-up lake. The early nineteenth-century Protestant church tower is another eye-catcher and was used as a marker in point-to-point races in the days of the Kilkenny Hunt.

The Walled Garden of the big house is entered by an elaborate wrought-iron Gothic gate, which leads through further Gothic trellised arches that are linked by little chains and support climbing roses. These are surrounded by overgrown old apple trees, Irish yews, and thick box hedges.

In the 1790s two brothers, John and Richard Power, lived at Kilfane. They used to enjoy taking their guests on the two-mile walk or donkey ride to see the waterfall and eat supper in the *cottage ornée*. It was all part of the romantic ideal that linked a group of people who lived around Kilkenny in the late-eighteenth and early-nineteenth centuries. John started the Kilkenny Hunt in 1797, and Richard started the Kilkenny Theatre in 1802, which gave performances in aid of charity for a season every year for nearly 20 years. They were resident landlords, as were their neighbors and friends the Wrixon-Bechers, who lived at Creagh in West Cork but also had a house at Ballyglibin near Kilkenny. Other neighboring families included the Tighes at Woodstock, the Bushes at Kilmurray, the Trenches at Heywood, and the McMurrah-Kavanaghs at Borris.

After the Union between Ireland and England in 1800, when most landlords became absentee and migrated toward the grand life in London, this particular group of cultivated and patriotic individuals were determined to stay in their demesnes. They improved their estates and threw all their energies into creating a provincial society in Kilkenny that would rival that of Bath, England, at that time.

During the theater season, people would flock down from Dublin to go to the play by night and to hunt by day. The actors were the gentlemen from the neighboring houses and their guests, and the ladies were professional actresses. Several of the actresses later married their leading men, Bessy Dike marrying the poet Thomas Moore, and the great beauty and famous actress Eliza O'Neil marrying William Wrixon-Becher of Creagh in the church at Kilfane. Half the guests at the wedding wore hunting clothes, and the rest wore their theatrical fancy dress!

Thomas Moore acted at Kilfane, where plays were often put on in the big house. He was staying at Jenkinstown House for the Kilkenny theater season in the October of about 1805, where he saw a *Rosa chinensis* 'Old Blush' still in bloom, which, it is said, inspired him to write his love-lorn ballad, "The Last Rose of Summer." At the beginning of the 1800s, European gardeners did not have a wide choice of roses, and in particular they did not have many that would blossom throughout the summer into autumn and even, in mild years, into winter. The rose that Thomas Moore saw came to Europe from China in 1789, a derivative of two wild Chinese species, the true Chinese rose (*Rosa chinensis*) and the tea rose (*Rosa gigantea*). This new import had the ability to blossom in the Irish climate from late spring to mid fall, and when cross-bred with other roses, passed on this remarkable characteristic. Today, a direct descendant of this same Jenkinstown House old China rose 'Old Blush' is flowering in the National Botanic Garden in Glasnevin.

It was John Power's wife, Harriet, the niece of Henry Grattan, who landscaped these gardens. She had written a poem about two other gardens that she had designed at Mount Juliet, the home of the Earls of Carrick, and at Gurteen, where one of her daughters lived. Harriet created the *cottage ornée* and devised the plantings of the surrounding glen. The cottage would probably have been used most between the 1790s and 1820s, after which the Powers visited it less and less often. Finally, left to its own devices, the area was overtaken by the forest and completely forgotten. In 1988, no one alive had heard of the cottage or garden. The big house was still there, and what had been the Kilfane Dower House in the middle of a wood was for sale.

Nicholas Mosse, the famous potter from nearby Bennettsbridge, and his American wife, Susan, came to look at it, and, having seen the house, went to walk around the woods and immediately fell in love with the place. They bought the house and started work on the upper section of the garden, having no idea at the time that the second part existed. But when Jeremy Williams, the architect, came to dinner in 1990 and told them that he had seen watercolors in the Royal Society of Antiquaries of Ireland of a *cottage ornée* and waterfall, they determined to find and restore them. They began to explore, hacking back the laurels, and almost at once they found paths. Gradually a flight of stone steps emerged, leading down into the chasm

Opposite top: A distorting concave mirror called "Faeries Gate," made in 1995 by Sean Mulcahy, creates the illusion that the long narrow Victorian fern-edged path stretches away to infinity.

Opposite bottom: "Descending Vessel Kilfane," made by David Nash in 1996, is a piece of sculpture in which a pointed arrow appears to be coming up out of a tree. This was especially commissioned by Susan Mosse.

Below: This hypnotically comtemplative water sculpture, named "Vessel," is by William Pye. Installed in 1998, it stands in a glade near the house.

Bottom: If you tap the outside of the bronze drum of the "Vessel" the ripples spiral across the surface before plunging down smoothly into the goblet of the central funnel.

through which the river flowed, cascading from pool to pool along the glen. This is the same river that had to fill the big pond at Kilmurry (home of the incorruptible Charles Kendal Bushe in the eighteenth century, and where the garden painter Mildred Anne Butler lived at the end of the nineteenth century), and the ornamental lake in the garden at Kilfane. And then, having stumbled across the river, they came upon heaps of stones and two walls with laurel growing out of the stonework, with the remains of a porch standing where the cottage had been in the painting. When Nick found the ornamental pebblework pavement that runs around the edge of the cottage, he knew that he had uncovered the footprint of the building. Using the watercolors as reference, the Mosses gradually restored the cottage.

It seemed at first as though the waterfall had completely vanished. However, shortly afterwards the Mosses discovered the dried-up canal that had been built in the 1790s to create the waterfall, diverting the stream for a mile and allowing the water to tumble over the cliff beside the cottage. Not only had Harriet Power conceived the cottage, she must also have envisioned that it needed a waterfall to complete the romantic landscape. While the Powers owned all the required land for their Romantic Garden, it took protracted negotiations over several years to enable the Powers to buy the land and restore the canal to its original function, which was quite a feat of engineering even today, let alone nearly 200 years ago.

This restored *cottage ornée* is the oldest one of its kind in Ireland and, as with the Swiss Cottage at Cahir Park, was copied from the ideas of the French Queen, Marie Antoinette. Bored with the formalities and the routine of the French Court, she had the idea of building a country village where she and her friends could play at living in simple rusticity. The Queen's fantasy of rural life, called *Le Hameau*, was built in the grounds of the Petit Trianon at Versailles. All the buildings were thatched and the outer walls covered in trellis. This must have been the direct inspiration for these beautiful Irish cottages. Maybe the Kilfane cottage inspired the world-famous Ladies of Llangollen, Lady Eleanor Butler and Miss Sarah Ponsonby, who escaped from the grandeur of their unhappy homes near Kilfane to live together in a rural idyll in a cottage in Wales.

This romantic garden, with its waterfall and restored garden building, is of particular Irish interest historically, as it sheds light on the lives of a group of gifted and artistic people in the late-eighteenth and early-nineteenth-century – men and women, who were all, in one way or another, to play an important part in the cultural and intellectual life of their country. The discovery of Harriet Power as an unsung eighteen-century garden designer, and the replanting of the glen and restoration of the *cottage ornée* are perfect examples of the stories Kilfane has to tell. These, combined with the Mosses' twentieth-century vision of their atmospheric plant and sculpture garden melting into the surrounding wild woods of Kilfane, brings this lost romantic garden, with a long, albeit fractured, history, to life again.

Plan of Kilfane Glen and Waterfall

1. Grotto
2. Waterfall
3. Rustic Bridge
4. Stream Nore
5. Cottage Ornée
6. Mr Butler's Bridge
7. Pine Island
8. Stone Steps to Valley
9. Steps to Cockpit

KILLRUDDERY
COUNTY WICKLOW

The approach to Killruddery through a row of modern houses offers no clue that you are about to enter the most complete seventeenth-century garden in Ireland, and one of the most important surviving gardens of its type in the whole of England and Ireland. Set among the peaks of the Large and Small Sugar Loaf Mountains in County Wicklow, Killruddery has always been known as the "Big House" of the busy seaside town of Bray. In 1618, it was granted to the Norman-English Sir William Brabazon (later the first Earl of Meath). His grandson Edward, the fourth Earl, as part of the newly rich colonial aristocracy, was an enthusiastic follower of fashions – and this extended to his gardens. After the devastation caused by the English Civil War, Ireland looked to France (where the monarchy had just been restored) for inspiration. In 1684, the fourth Earl employed a noted French gardener, Monsieur Bonet, who was inspired by King Louis XIV's garden designer, Andre Le Nôtre, at Versailles.

The idea for the twin canals that stretch down the garden from the house at Killruddery came from Le Nôtre's canals at the Château de Courances, 30 miles south of Paris. At Killruddery, these inky black *miroirs d'eaux* (water mirrors), measuring 550 feet in length, were also stocked with fish for the house. There is no known English or Irish precedent for these canals, although the gardens at Antrim Castle, which were planted at the same time, contain a single canal that has recently been restored.

The fourth Earl had obviously been gripped by gardening fever, as an advertisement published in 1711 highlighted Killruddery's new summerhouse and a "pleasure garden, cherry garden, kitchen garden, New Garden, Wilderness, gravel walks, and bowling green." It also mentioned that the garden was walled, that it had many fruit trees and that the canals were full of carp and tench. In keeping with the spirit of the times, Killruddery constituted a physical expression of the fourth Earl's status and wealth, and was intended to dazzle and impress friends and rivals alike. It was conceived as a "garden of entertainment," with different garden "rooms" to be used as extensions of the house in the style of the English "Elizabethan Renaissance." A few features, such as the Ace of Clubs pond, have disappeared completely, but the simple plan of the demesne which was drawn up between 1740–1750 is still perfectly evident today.

In Seventeen Hundred and Forty and Four,
The Fifth of December ... I think 'twas no more,
At Five in the morning by most of our Clocks,
We rode from Killruddery, to try for a Fox.

Previous page, main picture: A pensive statue gazes through the autumn leaves of the circular beech hedge that encloses the stone pond in the Wilderness.

Previous page, detail: The leaves of the Ginkgo biloba, *or maidenhair, tree that stands in a sheltered position within one of the Angles.*

So wrote Thomas Mozeen, a friend of the fourth Earl, and a well-known actor and keen huntsman, in his famous ballad, "The Killruddery Hunt" in 1744. A primitive oil painting (c. 1740) celebrating this hunt still hangs at Killruddery, depicting hounds and huntsmen streaming across the landscape, with the original house and garden layout showing the "Angles". These are shown on the painting on the eastern side of the canals; the great radiating hedges of beech, hornbeam, and yew which are planted in the shape of a *patte d'oie* (foot of the goose).

Nearly a century later, during the 1820s, the tenth Earl, with his architects Richard Morrison and Francis Morrison, and his son William Vitruvius Morrison, turned the house around a half-circle so it now faces north, and changed it from the Killruddery seen in the hunting painting into a Jacobean-revival palace, of which a large part was pulled down in 1953.

The twin canals flank a central walkway, leading to a circular pond with a single jet of water. Farther on, a narrow canal takes the same curve and then runs westward beyond the hidden ditch, forming a break between the garden and what used to be the fourth Earl's deer park. The double Linden Avenue starts midway across the park and continues over the crown of the hill, while belts of beechwood on each side of the Linden Avenue rise up towards the slopes of Small Sugar Loaf Mountain. The eastern side of the garden, which was bounded by the old road to Bray, is subdivided into three parts. One area used to have a maze, now gone, and another a bowling green, now planted with silver birch. The surviving Angles take up the third part. On the western side of the canals lies the Wilderness (a French *bosquet*) with the Sylvan Theatre and the Beech Pond Circle.

Below left: Sheep graze in the old deer park beneath the majesty of the double Linden Avenue. A single jet of water from the fountain rises directly in line with the vista.

Below: Twin canals lead the eye into the landscape and add a touch of quietly formal serenity; green leaves reflect against the pale blue sky.

Above: A bird's-eye view of the house at Kilruddery embraced by the trees. The peak of the Small Sugar Loaf Mountain can be seen beneath the approaching cloud formation. The formal garden stretching away from the house is hinted at, but enticingly hidden.

Within the complicated formal design, it is fascinating to see how 300 years of growth have filled in and blurred, but never lost, the symmetry and straight lines of the original plan. Walking through the Angles of high clipped hedges of beech and hornbeam with beech sentinels at the end of each *allée* and perimeter walls of yew at the end of each triangle, it is like being among the pieces of the most elegant puzzle. Statues stand at the intersections, and there is a vista from each that is closed by an ancient tree, such as a huge holly or Scots pine. A cast-iron nymph signals one intersection, which looks on to the vivid green grass in one direction and to the black water of the canal in another. Each Angle offers peace and seclusion between the high hedges. Sometimes the Angles have just a single tree planted in the middle, a *Ginkgo biloba* or a modest *Euchryphia* x *nymansensis*.

On the eastern side, you meet a cagelike circle of giant yews with their branches meeting high above your head. The yew cloisters lead to what was once the bowling green, where specially selected and graded grasses were used to make sure the ball rolled true. The sunken lawn was surrounded by high grass terraces where spectators could sit comfortably and view the progress of the game. From here you can walk up the hill on your left through the beech trees, to the top of the rocky outcrop that stands to the east of the house. Squirrels race over the grass banks, holly bushes grow among the rhododendron, and the sun shines through the clouds of gnats under the chestnut trees. On the top of the rock where gorse and ferns flourish, you can see the house, sheltered by a ring of surrounding hills in a tapestry of fields. The town of Bray stretches away to the right. In the mown grass

Above: These trees in the full glory of their autumn color stand to the east of the house in the clearing below the rock. They are in front of where the Elizabethan entrance once was, before the house was rotated in the 1820s.

clearing at the foot of the rock, there is a sprawling strawberry tree (*Arbutus unedo*), just as at home here as in its native haunts around the lakes of Killarney.

The receipts and plant lists – all in spidery handwriting – from the years after 1731 when the sixth Earl married Juliana Prendergast offer fascinating evidence of the history of the garden at this exciting time. The lists mention 31 different carnations bought from Mr. Bacon in the first year. In other years there are 20 kinds of carnations, nearly 70 in another, and 42 in a third. In 1736, there were 74 Irish and 69 English varieties of auricula. There are also lists of ranunculus and tulips being shipped from Holland in 1739, tulips from Lille and Brussels in 1740, and hyacinths from Haarlem and Leyden in 1754. The garden was in its heyday at this time, as the flower books of the day testify. Indeed, some of Samuel Dixon's ravishing prints of flowers and birds were dedicated to the Countess of Meath. It is thought that, before gardening fashion banished all color and flowers to the walled garden, there was a

Below: The famous Killruddery Angles with high hedges of yew, full-grown lindens, and an autumnal Venus bathed in the glory of the morning light.

parterre linking the front of the house to the canals, and that many of these flowers were grown as bedding plants in between low box hedges. They would not have been planted in masses as in Victorian times, however, but rather as single specimens.

Juliana must often have wandered in the groves of the Wilderness, thinking about her garden, and planning who would be coming to enjoy it. If she walked through the wood, she would have emerged facing a tall beech circular hedge with arched niches and clipped "windows." At the center there is a round stone pond with a fountain. The hedge is formed from a double row of beech with a secret path through the middle. On an fall day, with the crackle of the dry leaves underfoot and the eerie-looking entwined and tortured branches above, you feel as if you are walking through an illustration in a fairy story. The dying sun skirts over the russet leaves of the hedge and pierces the darkness of the wood, where a stricken gladiator on a plinth stands in a circle of ancient yews.

Top: A nineteenth-century cast-iron statue of an angelic beauty that the eleventh Earl of Meath bought and placed in the garden at some time in the 1850s or 1860s.

Above: The glades and the clearings of the Wilderness are peopled by statues. Here, a cast-iron goddess on her stone plinth appears at the corner at the joining of two paths seen through the dappled shade of bosky woodland.

Above: The fountains in the pond are stilled and golden beech leaves herald the approach of fall, welcomed by the graceful nymphs that guard the pathway.

By the 1820s, with the tenth Earl at Killruddery, the formal layout of the garden had come to be admired for its durability, with all visitors remarking on its antiquity. The tenth Earl bought and placed around the garden the cast-iron statues of gods and goddesses signed by Barbezat et Cie, Val D'Osne, and F. Kahle of Potsdam. Near the Beech Pond Circle stands the most poetic of all auditoriums, the Sylvan Theatre, with its curved, shorn seats carved out of the banks of grass enclosed within a high bay laurel hedge. Moss-covered stone faces of comedy and tragedy lie on the ground as though waiting for the play to begin, and the tenth Earl wrote that "acting had constantly taken place in this Sylvan Theatre, both in his, and his father's time, private theatricals being then much in vogue; dramatic parties were made up and then invited from one country house to another." The idea much appealed to one visitor, Sir Walter Scott, who used it in *St. Ronan's Well.* The theater's grass banks give way to a lawn with a yew tree that is so old that its bark looks like folds of fabric. Birdsong and the sound of a fountain nearby draw you toward the rose beds. A small Ornamental Victorian Dairy is smothered in clematis and a huge old *Magnolia grandiflora* spreads across the west-facing wall of the house.

In 1846, during the eleventh Earl's occupation of Killruddery, the garden was fully restored by the landscape gardener Daniel Robertson. A conservatory, designed by the architect William Burn, was built in 1852. It is said that the delicate lacelike stone parapet was copied from Lady Meath's tiara before it was sold to pay for the building work. Over the next century, a rock garden was planted on an outcrop of rock to the east of the house, and rose beds and hedges on a smaller scale were added near the Ornamental Victorian Dairy on the west. The gardens were kept in good order until a lack of gardening help after World War II meant that hedges and paths became overgrown.

In 1951, the Earl and the Countess of Meath returned to live in Killruddery and were faced with an enormous house full of dry rot, heavy duties to pay and an overgrown garden. "It was very gloomy" remembers Lady Meath, "the roof was leaking everywhere." To start with, they decided to pull down one wing with the help of the architect, Claude Phillimore. The former dining room with its view of the hill was made into a terrace, its decorative edging recycled from a dismantled gable.

When Lord and Lady Meath first came back to live here, they didn't have a gardener at all, and there were dandelions growing all over the walks. "We beheaded them and poured sodium chlorate and would weed all around the long ponds with watering cans, and by degrees the paths came back. We grew raspberries and tried to sell the vegetables at market. We never stopped working in the summers." For the first time, in the fall of 1997, they were able to clip the Angles and now have two full-time gardeners who do the clipping once a year in winter.

The continued existence of the gardens at Killruddery is a tribute to all those who have been in charge of them over the years. They stand and flourish as testament to the planning and design skills of the fourth Earl, and the contrast between the man-made formality of the gardens and the wild untamed sides of the Sugar Loaf Mountains, visible from all parts of the garden, is still as dramatic today as it was three centuries ago.

Below: The playing fountains, seen through the beech trees, can only be heard when you are standing inside the circular hedge.

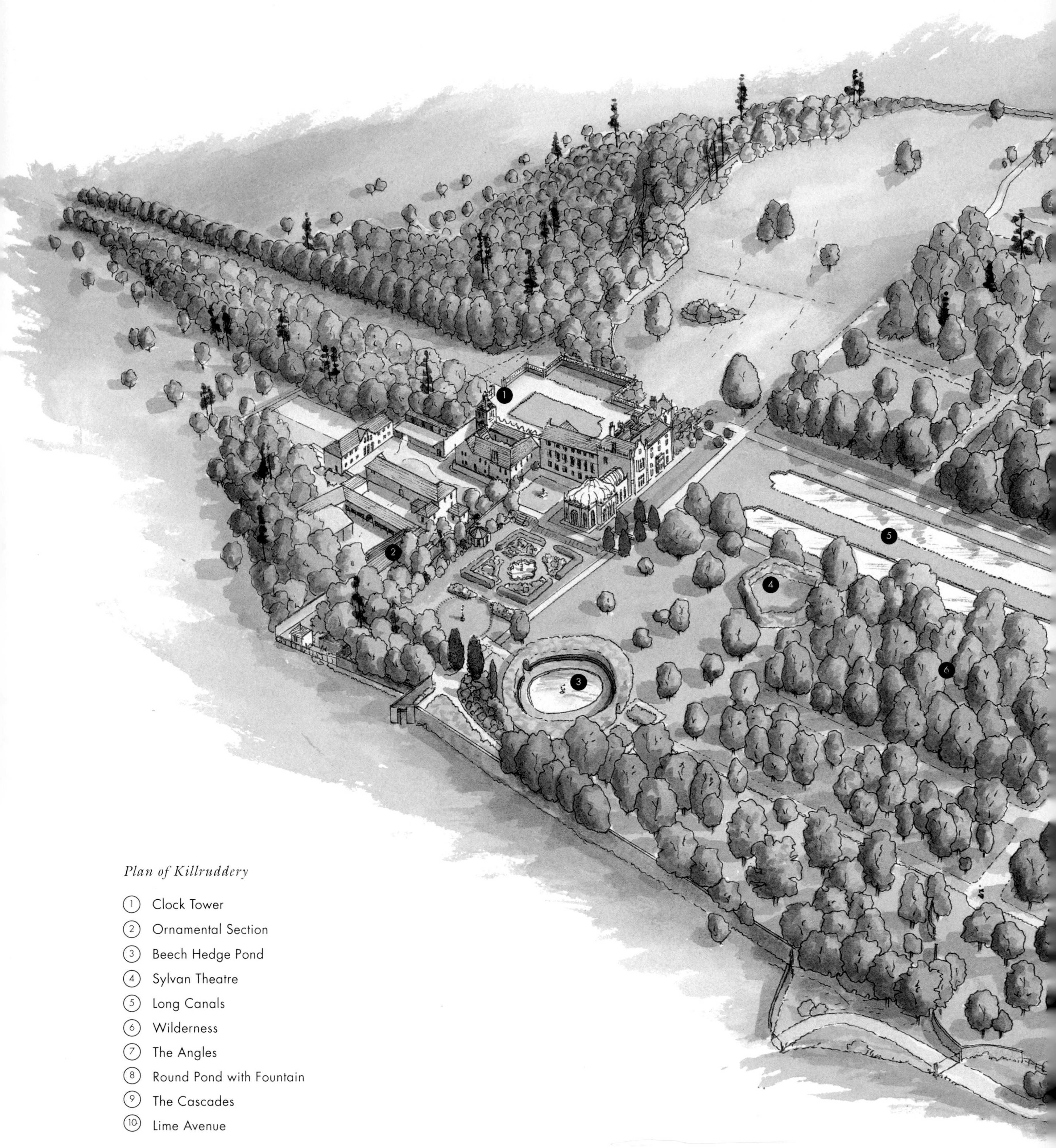

Plan of Killruddery

1. Clock Tower
2. Ornamental Section
3. Beech Hedge Pond
4. Sylvan Theatre
5. Long Canals
6. Wilderness
7. The Angles
8. Round Pond with Fountain
9. The Cascades
10. Lime Avenue

MOUNT STEWART
COUNTY DOWN

The house and gardens of Mount Stewart are situated on the edge of Strangford Lough on the western shore of the narrow peninsula of the Ards in County Down. The garden was created by Edith, Lady Londonderry, a capricious lady of dauntless energy and enthusiasm, who at first sight described her husband's ancestral mansion as being "the darkest, dampest, saddest place I ever stayed in." Before long, though, she was to transform the grounds into a whimsical and extravagant garden reminiscent of a Lewis Carroll tale.

The 80-acre site is characterized by an almost overwhelming conglomeration of different styles of architecture and planting, that is saved from confusion only by the sense that there has been a single hand with a dashing touch at the helm throughout. It is heartening to see that so much of what she created is still in such good shape, with an extraordinary number of tender plants flourishing.

Previous page, main picture: An arcade of closely clipped Leyland cypresses is one of the most unusual features in Mount Stewart, one of the jewels in the crown of the National Trust in Northern Ireland. Jerusalem sage and the gray, pointed foliage of Kniphofia caulescens *complement each other, while a red-leaved cabbage palm stands aloof.*

Previous page, detail: Nasturtiums planted in a stone trough provide a splash of color.

Above: The harp is the emblem of Ireland. This one is formed from yew and stands within a shamrock-shaped compartment.

When Lady Londonderry came to live here in 1919, she immediately swept away the holm oaks that made the house dark and airless and launched a program of nonstop planning, clearing, designing, and planting that lasted until 1927. Gertrude Jekyll sent over a plan for the Sunken Garden, and with this in her hand, Lady Londonderry set about reviewing all she knew about gardening and garden design. The Boboli Gardens in Florence, the Villa Gamberaia at Setignano, the Villa Farnese at Caparola, not to mention her mother's garden at Dunrobin Castle in Scotland, were all enthusiastically plundered for inspiration. The sheer scale of the overall design and the intensity of the planting is awesome even today, and Lady Londonderry was assisted by a small army of builders and gardeners. This was during the difficult period of demobilization after World War I, and landlords were being asked to employ as many extra people as possible. At least 20 men were allocated to Mount Stewart, and taking advantage of this opportunity, Lady Londonderry was able to forge ahead with her spectacular plans.

Realizing the benefits of the climate that the gardens enjoyed was key to their development. "The really exciting and important thing about Mount Stewart was discovering the climate, and this, I think, I may claim to have done," she wrote proudly. As Mount Stewart is situated in the northeast of Ireland, it has the major benefit of enjoying more sunshine and less rain than other parts of the country. It is also essentially frost-free. When Lady Londonderry started the garden, she had no idea that the Gulf Stream, which feeds the 17-mile-long Strangford Lough, would make it possible for her to grow the many half-hardy shrubs and more tender *Rhododendron* species that one would usually expect to grow in a greenhouse. Mimosa trees, Banksian roses, the Chilean bell flower (*Lapageria rosea*) and countless other tender plants thrive happily outdoors. So narrow is the space between the head of Strangford Lough and that of Belfast Lough that Mount Stewart experiences island conditions – the atmosphere is humid, and in hot weather, there are very heavy dews at night. All these factors combine to bring about an extraordinary rate of growth, and throughout the garden the groves of eucalypts, rows of cabbage palms (*Cordyline australis*), and spiky-leaved palms create an atmosphere that you might expect to find in a garden in the Azores.

Two advisers encouraged Lady Londonderry to be adventurous and grow the tenderest plants: Sir John Ross-of-Bladensburg, who lived at Rostrevor in County Down and made a marvelous collection of trees and rare shrubs from all over the world on the slopes of a hill overlooking Carlingford Lough, and Sir Herbert Maxwell of Montreith in Wigtownshire, who also had a wonderful garden packed with rare species. She also took advice from Gertrude Jekyll and corresponded with plant collectors Clarence Elliott, George Forrest, and Frank Kingdon Ward. She ordered plants from nurseries across Europe, while her woody plant collection was dominated by Southern Hemisphere species.

To cheer and enliven the surroundings of her husband's sober Georgian house, she threw out suites of garden rooms on the south, west, and east fronts, all sheltered from the lough by a proscenium of trees. Without any view or vista through to the beautiful waters of the lough, Lady Londonderry succeeded in creating an enclosed, exotic and lush, almost dreamlike world.

Entering the garden on the west side, you walk through an ironwork gate flanked by stone pillars, with the sinuous necks of swans emerging from crowns, the family crest. The Sunken Garden was one of Lady Londonderry's first projects, and it is surrounded on three sides by a tall clipped hedge of Leyland cypress, which is so feathery and such a bright green that it looks like a fur carpet. The heavy stone pergola is hung with potato vines (*Solanum*), clematis, fuchsias, California lilacs (*Ceanothus*), and *Rosa gigantea* from western China and northern Burma, as well as having uncommon and delicate slipperworts growing through the paved path below. Fifty-year-old bay trees, bought in Leghorn, are sculpted into domes and grown in pots on the terrace. Four herbaceous beds, carved out of the grass, are filled in summer with dephiniums, lilies, day lilies, and phlox, and each is bordered by two different hedges meeting at the corners of tightly clipped boxwood and bay. Scattered throughout are tall tree heathers, *Erica arborea* and *E. lusitanica*, while in spring, borders of flame-colored azaleas light up the greenery.

The journey through the gardens is compelling. Irresistible glimpses lead you from one compartment to the next, each one more enticing and exotic than the last. One of the most original compartments is designed in the shape

Below: Roses and honeysuckles clamber up this stone-and-wood pergola. The splashes of scarlet are provided by nasturtiums and Peruvian lilies.

Above: The plant collection at Mount Stewart is outstanding. Here the red Crocosmia masoniorum *is combined with the slender spires of white-flowered loosestrife.*

of a shamrock and surrounded by a seven-foot hedge of English yew, with two scissor-clipped topiary crowns and topiary figures of a family hunting party chasing each other along the top of the hedge. The figures were copied and adapted from Queen Mary Tudor's fourteenth-century psalter. "All the weird animals, devils, boats, and birds are drawn in the margins of the leaves. All we did was substitute members of the family for the originals," writes Lady Londonderry nonchalantly. The symbol of Ulster, a huge red hand, is planted in the gravel in *Begonia* 'Red Devil.' Behind this stands a yew tree clipped into flat, round table tops, on the topmost tier of which stands a topiary harp, the symbol of Ireland. The Londonderrys believe themselves to be descended from the first O'Neill, who, in a desperate race with a rival clan across the Irish Sea from Scotland, cut off his right hand and threw it onto Ulster's shore to lay claim to the country. Plants for winter interest grow in the beds behind this Celtic showstopper: camellias, mahonias, sweet box (*Sarcococca*), *Viburnum* x *bodnantense*, and the graceful coral-stemmed Japanese maple, *Acer palmetum* 'Senkaki.' There are also roses nearby, including 'Emily Gray' and 'Lady Hillingdon,' tea trees from New Zealand (*Leptospermum scoparium*) and *Hydrangea involucrata* and *H. scandens chinensis*.

The Lily Wood, next on the agenda, is in true Robinsonian style. A winding path leads past delicate rhododendrons, tree ferns more than 12 feet high, lots of lilies, such as *L. martagon* and 'Shuksan,' the Chilean firebush

Above: Dodos guard Noah's Ark while griffins look on. The statuary at Mount Stewart is pure fun. And, true to the principles nurtured by Gertrude Jekyll (who helped Lady Londonderry design this garden), plant colors are carefully combined for maximum effect.

(*Embothrium coccineum*) from Rostrevor, eucryphia, and various creepers growing up pine trees. There are blue poppies, primulas, hostas, and trilliums, as well as the jealously prized *Cardiocrinum giganteum*, the stately Himalayan lily that reaches over 10 feet and has huge white trumpet-shaped flowers.

From here, it is all too tempting to move straight into the Spanish Garden, but in order to realize the full extent of Lady Londonderry's vision, you should approach this garden from the front of the house with the Spanish-tiled loggia as your focus. The shape of the herbaceous beds in the center of the adjacent Italian Garden, which runs the full length of the house, was copied from her mother's garden at Dunrobin Castle in Scotland. The idea for the accompanying stonework came from the Villas Gamberaia and Farnese. The high-clipped yew hedges of the Boboli Gardens were the inspiration for the rather more spindly version in Leyland cypress that frames the loggia. Pairs of columns are topped by heraldic griffins, urns, and herms. Lady Londonderry did not approve of boxwood, so the beds are edged in a mixture of colors, using purple berberis, white heather, blue rue, golden thuja, and silvery hebe. Two stone ponds filled with water lilies and surrounded by lilies and hostas are a complement to the surrounding beds of silvery mauve on the one side and a welcome alternative to the strong orange and reds on the other. Finally, there is a double row of New Zealand cabbage palms (*Cordyline australis*) marching down the middle.

Above: A view of the main formal parterre at the south front of Mount Stewart. The dominant colors are "hot" dark reds and oranges and yellows.

Opposite above: The centerpiece and focus of the front view from the house is the small Spanish tiled loggia in the Spanish Garden below the semicircular flight of stone steps. The design of this garden was inspired by a plasterwork ceiling by Robert Adam that Lady Londonderry originally saw in the Mansion House in London.

Opposite below: Looking back from the parterre to the terrace of the house itself across the fountain playing in the round stone pond. The walls of the house are hung with creepers, and the layout and shapes of the beds in the parterres were copied from those at Dunrobin Castle, Scotland.

Lady Londonderry was not only an avid gardener, but also a famous political hostess. During the World War I, she had formed the Ark Club at Londonderry House, which provided an oasis in London for her family and close friends – soldiers, politicians, poets, artists, and composers – to meet informally. The members of the club all took the names of animals extant or extinct, and many of them are represented on the Dodo Terrace, cast in concrete by a local craftsman in memory of the club. Lady Londonderry was Circe the Sorceress, Winston Churchill was Winston the Warlock, Ramsay MacDonald was Hamish the Hart, and so on. Four dodos on pillars guard the ark underneath the eucalypts, and other curious-looking creatures on their plinths along the walls eye the intruder with baleful half-human expressions.

The rhododendrons on the Dodo Terrace shelter the next compartment, which is the Mairi Garden, named after Lady Mairi Vane-Tempest-Stewart (later Viscountess Bury, the Londonderrys' daughter.). It is planted in the shape of a Tudor rose and filled with blue and white plants, such as agapanthus, campanulas, and *Galtonia candicans*, as well as white fuchsias, buddleias, and Bourbon roses. In the center is a fountain dedicated to the "Mary Mary Quite Contrary" of the nursery rhyme, as a reminder of the days when the youngest daughter of the house was put here to sleep in her buggy next to the summerhouse and dovehouse. Wafts of resin fill the air from the 120-foot *Eucalyptus globulus*, of which this garden has the most concentrated planting in northern Europe. They were grown from seeds brought back by Theresa, Lady Londonderry, from South Africa in 1894.

Although one could be excused for thinking that the tour was now over as a wisteria-covered tunnel leads to the parking lot, in fact one would be missing the informal walks up into the slopes at the other side of the house. Here you can take the Lake Walk, passing the large artificial lake laid out in the 1840s. This is where you would have once looked down across an open park to the house with the lough beyond. Now, on the path from the drive, there are rhododendrons, azaleas, magnolias, and a group of *Cordyline indivisa* from New Zealand with their swordlike leaves. The banks of the lake are decorated with Japanese ornaments collected by the Londonderrys on a tour of Japan. Above the lake, you can see the distant turrets of the family burial ground in a walled enclosure called in Irish *Tir-n'an Oge* or "The Land of the Ever Young." The great white stag that is reputed to bear the souls of the departed to heaven can be seen standing in a tree-lined glade.

Another path leads through a wood of beech trees. Turning a corner, in front of you stands a perfect copy of the Tower of Andronicus Cyrrhestes in Athens. Built by the architect James "Athenian" Stuart in 1780, this is the Temple of The Winds, designed as a banqueting house and made of pale Scrabo stone with floors of fir found in the bogs on the estate. It is arguably the most beautiful garden building in Ulster. It gazes out serenely over the blue waters of Strangford Lough, secure in its chastely perfect proportions and untouched by the excitements of a later age.

Today, Mount Stewart is one of the most important gardens in Ireland. It is the most complete example of the compartmental style of gardening of its date in the country. Lady Londonderry died in 1959, but her daughter, Viscountess Bury, lives in the house, which along with the garden, now belongs to and is cared for by the National Trust. Under the present head gardener, Nigel Marshall, direct acquisition of seeds from America and Australia has again become a vital part of the garden's regeneration. The plant collection has expanded and been improved with new plantings, thus keeping Lady Londonderry's imaginative spirit alive.

Plan of Mount Stewart

1. Mairi Garden
2. Dodo Terrace
3. Fountain Walk
4. Spanish Garden
5. Italian Garden
6. Peace Garden
7. Lily Wood
8. River
9. Memorial Glade
10. Sunken Garden
11. Shamrock Garden
12. Lake Walk
13. Lake
14. The Hill
15. Temple of the Winds
16. Jubilee Avenue Walk
17. Rhododendron Wood
18. Ladies' Walk

MOUNT USHER
COUNTY WICKLOW

Tucked into the landscape between the hills of County Wicklow and the sea lie the gardens of Mount Usher. They are sheltered by the hills of the valley of the silvery River Vartry as it flows down from the Devil's Glen. When the famous eighteenth-century traveler and diarist Mrs. Delany visited her friend, Mrs. Usher of Mount Usher, in 1752, she reported on the beauty of the countryside. "Fine meadows, shady lanes, one side skirted by mountains and hills of various shapes, diversified with cultured fields, bushes and rocks and some woods, on the other side a beautiful prospect of the sea and the roads like gravel walks, the hedges enriched with golden furze and silver May. This country is particularly famous for arbutus (the strawberry tree) and myrtles, which grow in common ground and flourish as in Cornwall." One day they called on Mr. Tighe, whose garden at his demesne Rossannagh was divided from Mr. Usher's by "a very pretty clear river: he came in his boat to waft us over."

Previous page, main picture: Rhododendron barbatum, *a native of the Himalayas, is just one of the hundreds of rhododendrons at Mount Usher, a garden in which the sound of running water is always present.*

Previous page, detail: Mahonia *make excellent winter-flowering shrubs. The genus is named for the Irish-American horticulturist Bernard McMahon.*

Right: A happy combination – an azalea and some candelabra primulas blooming in spring.

Opposite: Bluebells and daffodils form a carpet under Acer griseum, *a splendid small maple renowned for its peeling cinnamon-red bark.*

When the Ushers of Mount Usher died or moved away, the Tighes must have bought their property. Mr. Tighe then leased it to a miller, who first ran a tuck mill for finishing woollen cloth and then a corn mill using the water from the river to turn the mill wheel. Time passed, and in the 1860s, Edward Walpole, a successful Dublin businessman involved in the linen trade, appeared on the scene. He was staying in Hunter's Hotel, a cream-colored Georgian house that stands approximately two miles from the garden. Edward and the owner of the mill, Sam Sutton, became fast friends, and he returned often to enjoy the mountain air and walk in the surrounding hills. Soon he was staying at the miller's house rather than the hotel and had grown to love the wooded valley, so much so that when the miller's lease expired in 1868, Edward took it over. He acquired the one acre and 11 perches that began his family's relationship with Mount Usher, which was to last 112 years. He wasn't to know it immediately, but the site had almost perfect conditions for growing the tenderest of plants. The soil is alluvial gravel or sand overlaying patches of heavy clay, and is lime free. The rainfall averages 36 inches a year and frost is rare.

To start with, in place of the potatoes that grew in front of the house, Edward planted flowers, and to his astonishment, everything he planted flourished. He soon bought more land and enlarged the property. In 1875, when he was 77, Edward Walpole gave the property to his three sons. It was the combination of their skills that was to make Mount Usher a perfect example of a Robinsonian garden. Edward and George were the gardeners, while Thomas, fascinated by civil engineering and architecture, was responsible for the planning of the waterworks and the bridges. They were succeeded by a grandson, E. Horace Walpole, one of the greatest Irish gardeners of his generation, and then in turn by his son Robert, who sold the property in 1980 to the present owner, Mrs. Madeleine Jay.

The Walpole brothers filled the garden with a number of unusual plants little tried in Ireland before, collected from nurseries all over the world. Seeds and plants came from Britain, France, Italy, and Germany, as well as New Zealand, Australia, Japan, and North America. The original book of introductions still exists, with lists of plants bought from the Vilmorin Nurseries in France and from Yokohama in Japan.

In the early 1880s, William Robinson was firing his first salvos against the stiff and formal Victorian ideal of planting in his book, *The English Flower Garden*. He visited Mount Usher and gave his seal of approval. He thoroughly agreed with the way the Walpoles were mixing exotic plants with the native trees and shrubs, allowing nature and the natural habit of each plant to dictate its situation and planting. Frederick Moore, the Director of the Royal Botanic Gardens in Glasnevin, visited the brothers in 1885 and saw at once that Mount Usher had the perfect soil, water, and climate to make an extraordinary garden. From then on, he kept them supplied with the names of new exotics and helped them to collect the rare plants that otherwise would have been difficult to find in Britain or Ireland at that time.

Above: The River Vartry is "stepped" by weirs, creating a pattern of still water and white foam.

Over the years, more land was bought, and in 1927, the freehold was purchased and the old mill pulled down. A modern house was then built, around which the gardens have grown to the present 20-acre site. The philosophy, passion, and knowledge of gardening, combined with a thorough understanding of the site and its conditions, were passed down through the generations of the Walpole family. Assistance was also provided by some of Ireland's leading horticulturalists. With the support of Mrs. Jay, the present head gardener, John Anderson, who trained at the National Botanic Gardens and at the Royal Botanic Gardens at Kew, is continually collecting and planting very much in the Walpole tradition. Today, the ever-increasing collection of trees and plants at Mount Usher, where planting began in 1868, are all sited in a continuation of Robinsonian principles without a jarring note.

Above: Sweet Gum with the last vestiges of its foliage, by the River Vartry.

The mature trees that form the bones of the garden are awe-inspiring. Some were planted as early as the 1880s, and they include the largest collection of Southern Hemisphere conifers in Ireland – there are 28 species, from the New Zealand kauri pine (*Agathis australis*) to the Prince Albert's yew (*Saxegothea conspicua*) from South America. There are superb specimens of northern conifers such as Montezuma's pine (*Pinus montezumae*) grown from seed and presented to Mount Usher in 1907 by Lord Wicklow, the handsome coffin juniper (*Juniperus recurva* var. *coxii*) from the China/Burma border, and Brewer's spruce (*Picea breweriana*) with its drooping branches.

Slender and graceful with their pale cream and gray trunks, the collection of Australian eucalypts contains about 50 different species, including the manna gum (*Eucalyptus viminalis*), the Tasmanian snow gum (*E. coccifera*), apple box (*E. bridgesiana*, formerly *E. stuartiana*), and alpine ash (*E. delegantensis*). There is also a comprehensive collection of southern beeches (*Nothofagus*), the most striking being the evergreens *N. menziesii*, the silver beech from New Zealand, and from Chile *N. nitida* (coigue de Chiloe) and *N. dombeyi* (coigue). In spring, the grass below is scattered with trout lilies and anemones, with fritillaries looking like small squares of checked voile that have been dropped in the grass. In early spring, the flowers and buds make a startling impression on the bare wood of leafless trees and shrubs. The pure white flowers of *Magnolia salicifolia* seem like bands of folded linen against its bare branches, and an early-flowering leafless cherry (*Prunus incisa*) has tiny flowers like pale pink shells. The Japanese magnolias, *M. kobus* and *M. obovata*, each have a brilliant central ruby boss of stamens, and *Primula megaseifolia* from the Black Sea coast of northern Turkey can be seen flourishing in a pocket on the river wall.

The River Vartry divides the garden, which is planted in long narrow strips along each of the river banks. The engineering brother, Thomas Walpole, strung a series of bridges over the river, replacing the earlier stepping stones, and laid out the trail of streams that weaves through the property. Ferns of every description grow on each side clinging to old tree trunks and stones.

When Mrs. Jay bought the property, she banned the use of chemicals. John Anderson explains: "Since we have stopped using them, we have got the thrushes and frogs back. In the autumn, the Vartry is full of herons, kingfishers, otters and wagtails, and sometimes ten-pound salmon." Rusty swamp cypresses (*Taxodium distinchum*), a spreading Persian ironwood tree (*Parrotia persica*), liquid amber (*Cercidiphyllum japonicum*), a golden larch

Below: The maple walk leading to the banks of the River Vartry. Wild birds, such as these mallards, are especially encouraged at Mount Usher.

(*Pseudolarix amabilis*), a New Zealand flax, mountain dogwood (*Cornus nuttallii*), and many more plants and trees lead the eye into the glades. Exotic plants have naturalized along the river banks, and myrtle, willow, and giant Chilean rhubarb seem to be weeping into the water.

The Maple Walk is at its most brilliant in the fall with the curling bark of *Acer griseum*, the striated stems of snakebark maples, and the red twigs of the coral-bark maple, *Acer palmatum* 'Senkaki.' Azaleas and rhodendendrons supply color in May, with *Rhododendron sinogrande* and *R. falconeri* flowering profusely, as well as the lavender-blue *R. augustinii* and the huge-flowered loderi hybrids. In summer and early autumn, the eucryphia collection is spectacular, with large clumps and avenues of the special Mount Usher hybrid with big white flowers, the result of a cross between *E. glutinosa* and *E. cordifolia*. Other summer delights are provided by *Hydrangea sargentiana*, *H. villosa*, and golden hypericums, escallonias, California lilacs (*Ceanothus*) and veronicas (*Hebe*). There are 20 acres of garden and perhaps 5,000 different plants. Two percent have come from South Africa, 50 percent from Asia, the Himalayas and China, eight percent from Australasia, eight percent from Europe, and 12 percent from North America.

When Mount Usher was for sale, Mrs. Jay bought the garden to save it. "So many beautiful things in Ireland disappear, and it would have been so awful if it had been lost," she tells me, and feels that her daring has been rewarded many times over. John Anderson is tireless in his support, and has a vigilant eye and passion for plants. This managed wilderness, combining exotics and old native favorites, gives this garden a life and spirit that makes it a joy to visit at any time of the year.

Below: The placid waters of the River Vartry reflect the glorious colors of graceful trees on a peaceful afternoon in the fall.

Plan of Mount Usher

1. Pond
2. Stream
3. Bridge
4. Old Millstone
5. Maple Walk
6. River Vartry
7. Azalea Walk
8. Bridge
9. Palm Walk
10. Nothofagus
11. Lime Walk

NATIONAL BOTANIC GARDENS
GLASNEVIN, DUBLIN

For more than 200 years the National Botanic Gardens have been at the forefront of Irish horticultural progress. Arriving there today, you turn off the main street and pass through chaste wrought-iron gates with two eighteenth-century lodges, one on each side of the path. It is like entering a different world altogether, leaving behind the streets of pink Victorian brick and the hustle and bustle of modern living. The feeling of being encompassed by a separate, yet demanding, discipline in a completely peaceful atmosphere is one to be savored.

The Botanic Gardens were started in 1795 by Dr. Walter Wade, a Dublin surgeon and male midwife. The petition to fund the gardens was pushed through the Irish Parliament by the Speaker of the day, John Foster, a keen collector of plants, agricultural improver, and tree planter at his estate, Collon, in County Louth. He was also a leading light in the Royal Dublin Society, which managed the garden with a grant from the government.

Previous page, main picture: The Curvilinear Range contains a collection of primitive cone-bearing cycads.

Previous page, detail: Detail of a cast-iron fluted acanthus capital on the Curvilinear Range.

Above: The Central Pavilion of Richard Turner's spectacular range of iron greenhouses. It was restored during the early 1990s and recommissioned in 1995 to celebrate the National Botanic Gardens' 200th anniversary.

There had been previous pleas to the government that the country needed a botanical garden for growing and studying medicinal plants, and promoting and improving plants used in agriculture and horticulture.

So, 27 acres were purchased in Glasnevin, a Dublin suburb, with the River Tolka forming the northern boundary. Delville, the idyllic garden that had belonged to Dean Delany and his wife, Mary, was nearby. Dean Delany had been a friend of the poet Thomas Tickell, the previous owner of the land, and it is said that Tickell had planted the old Yew Walk, which still stands today, in memory of his friend, Joseph Addison, the English essayist. It is this tangible connection with the past through its buildings, plants, and trees that gives the Botanic Gardens such an atmosphere of tranquility and romance.

Dr. Wade was elected the Dublin Society's Professor of Botany in 1796. Two years later, John Underwood became head gardener at the Botanic Gardens, and for the next 25 years, until Dr. Wade's death, they developed the basis of the plant collections. Standards then declined until Ninian Niven, a skilled gardener and designer, took over from Underwood in 1834. During his four years at Glasnevin, Niven breathed new life into the Gardens and was particularly interested in introducing new plants from overseas.

In 1838, David Moore was appointed curator, and under his direction the Botanic Gardens became world renowned, with Queen Victoria giving her seal of approval by visiting the Gardens in 1849. Between 1843 and 1870 the great Curvilinear Range of greenhouses was built, making it possible for tender exotics to flourish. In 1845, orchid seed germinated for the first time in Glasnevin; the late blight of the potato was ominously observed on August

20 of the same year. In 1854, the Aquatic House was erected to house the giant water lily (*Victoria amazonica*) from the Amazon. The first hybrid pitcher plants (*Sarracenia*) were raised around 1870. David Moore died in 1879 and was succeeded by his son, Frederick. Frederick Moore continued his father's excellent work, expanding the orchid and cycad collections, as well as continuing with the hybrid pitcher-plant breeding program. Under his direction the Gardens gained a reputation for cultivating "difficult" plants, and Glasnevin was considered superior to its sister botanic gardens at Kew and Edinburgh. Sir Frederick Moore and his wife, Phylis, were the undisputed king and queen of Irish horticulture. He retired in 1922 and was followed by several excellent curators, who consolidated his work and added to the collections with hardy trees and shrubs being introduced from the Far East.

Donal Synnott, who has worked at the institution for 28 years, is the present director, and the Gardens are undergoing a renaissance under the guardianship of Dúchas, the Department of Arts, Heritage, Gaeltacht and the Islands. Donal feels that the Gardens at the moment are an underutilized asset and is eager to bring them to a wider audience and, in particular, to encourage more Irish people to enjoy this great treasure.

As you enter the Botanic Gardens, you will see, at any time of day, gardeners tending the herbaceous beds. Here, as in the rest of the Gardens, Irish plants and trees are all carefully labeled with their Latin, English, and Irish names. Plants and trees stand singly or in family groups or beds, allowing previously unmade connections to become clear. On my visit, I was surprised to discover that columbines and delphiniums belong to the same family.

Ahead of you is the elegant Victorian Curvilinear Range of greenhouses designed and built by Richard Turner between 1843 and 1868. These have now been restored to their original glory by the Office of Public Works architect, Ciaran O'Connor. The sun gleams on the thin curved panes of glass, which fit into their cream-painted, wrought-iron casing with classical pillars and Victorian frill. Within, the potted cycads look mysterious beneath the arching spandrels of the roof in the vapor of a simulated tropical downpour.

To the right of the Curvilinear Range stand the Cactus and Fern Houses. Outside, the structures are ringed by arum lilies (*Zantedeschia aethiopica*), agapanthus, and libertia, and the lovely long-stemmed white bells of *Watsonia borbonica* subsp. *ardernei* from Cape Province in South Africa. The dry air of the Cactus House gives way to the dripping fernery in the Aquatic House, where the Jeremy Fisher-like, flat-cupped water-lily leaves of *Victoria amazonica* astonished the world when they were first shown in public in 1854. Ferns of every description line the artificial river gorge like a fairy grotto. The 400-year-old fern from the Royal Botanic Gardens in Melbourne that was presented to Trinity College, Dublin, in 1892, and then passed on to Glasnevin in 1969, looks completely at home among so many compatriots.

Today, the Great Palm House is sadly in need of repair. It was built in 1884 at a cost of $1200 and in great haste, because the previous house was so rickety it was virtually blown down in gales. The paint is peeling and the walls

Top: The handsome front entrance to the Great Curvilinear Range of cast-iron greenhouses with a tropical mist being simulated within.

Above: Modern technology now provides a fog-like mist so plants from tropical rainforests can be cultivated in the greenhouses.

Above: The giant leaves of Victoria amazonica *are said to be capable of bearing the weight of a baby. They are about four feet across. The flowers are pale pink but open only for one night. Growing with* Victoria amazonica *is another smaller tropical water lily with rose-pink flowers.*

are crumbling, yet the forest of subtropical palms and giant creepers still reaches to the roof. The Orchid House, just to the right of the Palm House, is filled with an ever-expanding collection, but, it too is under threat.

The Botanic Gardens has a three-year course teaching 150 students the academic and practical aspects of gardening. Sheltered by the Caucasian elm (*Zelkova carpinifolia*), there is an excellent library in a fine new building designed by Ciaran O'Connor. The National Herbarium (an archive for plants containing dried and documented specimens) contains over 600,000 examples of plants, including mosses, ferns, fungi, and seaweeds, and provides essential reference sources for scholarly study as well as for the naming of plants and maintaining the standards of horticultural exactitude. The botanical library

includes rare illustrated books, herbals dating from 1532, nursery catalogs,
complete runs of botanical magazines, fascinating early botanic photographs,
over 2,500 watercolor illustrations, and records from notable Irish plant
collectors, including Augustine Henry and Robert Lloyd Praeger.

To the left of the new library is the new Alpine House, built of Douglas fir
in the proper old-fashioned shape. There are pans of brightly colored alpines
in tightly flowering mounds on gravel beds. Tiny climbers with tendrils
clinging to a rock in a wet pan are labeled as coming from Dingle, Nepal,
North America, and Europe. Outside, alpines grow in beds within an enclosed
garden with climbers on the walls. The overall impression is one of freshness
and peace.

Above: The sharp spiky fronds of a palm leaf set against the decaying joints holding together the panes of glass in the Great Palm House.

Opposite above: The Great Palm House, built in 1884, is due to undergo a major restoration program.

Opposite center: Plume poppies (Macleaya microcarpa) and the California tree poppy (Romneya coulteri) in the Family Beds. These beds display plants related to one another. In the background is the Great Palm House.

Opposite below: The teak door of the Great Palm House – the wooden sashes are awaiting restoration.

Moving on, you pass a group of cherries and a bed of every kind of japonica (*Chaenomeles*), until you arrive at a solid swath of flowering bearded iris in spiky-leaved clumps of palest blue and violet darkening to purple flecked with yellow. Then a trellised circular walk held together by arches covered in different clematis encloses a group of magnolias. The plots of both the common and the exotic vegetables are enclosed by a tapestry hedge of different types of hollies. Another bed beyond is filled with pink-, white-, and purple-flowered *Weigela,* and then come the beds of deliciously scented mock orange, followed by the beds of species and garden varieties of *Deutzia* all planted together. A group of black locust (*Robinia pseudoacacia*) stands at the edge of the greenwood forest filled with oaks of every variety planted in shaded walks, separated from the Herb Garden by the Chinese Shrubbery.

Then there comes the glorious smell of pines, and you find yourself at one end of two, long, old-fashioned Edwardian perennial beds, each one at least 12 feet wide. A great swath of color sweeps up both sides of the path edged in boxwood, with flowers such as poppies, geraniums, lupines, tiny blue *Veronica pinnata*, delphiniums, and foxgloves. The sight is reminiscent of a painting by the Edwardian watercolorist, Mildred Anne Butler. All this part of the garden is so sheltered by the pines, some of them among the earliest introductions here, that there is never a gust of wind.

Reginald Farrer, the nineteenth-century plant collector, described the Rock Garden in the Botanic Gardens as a "Devil's Lapful." He wrote, "The plan is simplicity itself. You take a hundred or a thousand cartloads of bare, square-faced boulders. You next drop them all about absolutely anyhow; and you then plant things among them. The chaotic hideousness of the result is something to be remembered with shudders ever after." This seems rather a severe indictment of this period piece undergoing renewal as I write. Walking through the dappled groves of trees, another period piece, the "Chain Tent," catches your eye. Here you can sit under the "tent," which is covered in wisteria, and look out, through the light filtered through the wisteria, onto the clear pond dotted with pink, yellow, and white water lilies. Boxwood hedges hem in great clumps of wine-red peonies. A series of huge trees edge the water garden including the cucumber, hop, and tulip trees – hellebores, Solomon's seal, Siberian irises, montbretia, and day lilies all flourish far below their canopies. Across the River Tolka is a neatly laid out Rose Garden.

The Botanic Gardens at Glasnevin have always acted as the nerve center of Irish gardening. They received seeds from the great plant-hunters' expeditions to the Far East, collating and recording them, growing them, and then distributing them to interested gardeners all over the country. The Moore family's connection with Glasnevin spanned nearly a century from 1838 to 1922, and during that time there wasn't a serious gardener on this island who didn't benefit in some way from their help and advice. The great Irish plant collector, Augustine Henry, has many of the plants he discovered in central China represented at Glasnevin, including *Emmenopterys henryi*. An earlier plant collector, James Tweedie, corresponded with Ninian Niven and David Moore, and sent to Glasnevin in the 1840s the first pampas grass, *Cortaderia selloana,* from Argentina. Edward Madden sent back the giant lily *Cardiocrinum giganteum* and also the scented *Abelia triflora*, an original seedling of which still thrives in front of the Fern House. Ernest "Chinese" Wilson, who scoured China for the handkerchief tree, is remembered in the Chinese Shrubbery where plants still bear his collecting numbers. Some of the species rhododendrons that Charlotte Wheeler Cuffe painted in Burma in 1912 are doing well in the Curvilinear Range.

Among all the exotics that have been brought back at such cost of human endeavor from distant corners of the globe, there is perhaps one that no one would willingly pass by. Not loud or colorful, but just a small pink rose on a bush grown from a cutting taken from an Irish garden at Jenkinstown near Kilkenny. It is *Rosa chinesis* 'Old Blush', Thomas Moore's "Last Rose of Summer" (see page 159).

The director, who has spent so much of his life working in the National Botanic Gardens, must have the last word. "It is a complex place," he explains. "Gardens take a lifetime to make, and then they are hard to renew. In Victorian times, gardeners were skilled but not literate, but now our gardeners are fully qualified to take entire charge of collections. All the same, you can learn from the old gardeners. There was a period of resting, perhaps, when the general public weren't so interested, but gardening always went on in places like this – and now it has become a national pastime again." In the 1830s, 20,000 visitors came each year when there were only a couple of dozen seats for them to sit on after they had walked the three miles from Dublin. Now, visitor numbers are in excess of 100,000, and there are plenty of seats. Donal Synnott hopes that, with new facilities, such as a restaurant and lecture hall, and with the Curvilinear Range and Great Palm House restored, he can double the numbers of visitors to this splendid institution each year.

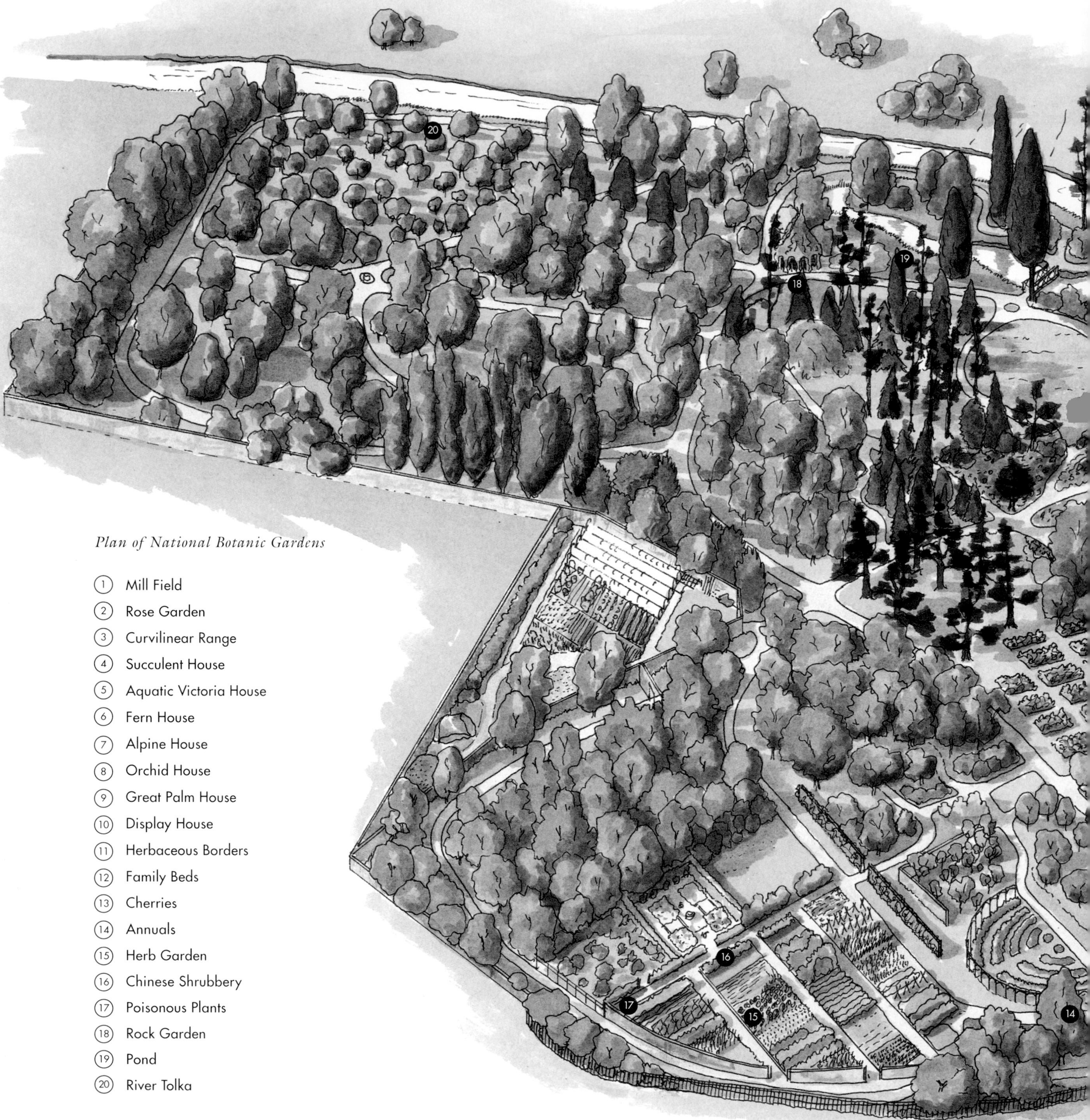

Plan of National Botanic Gardens

1. Mill Field
2. Rose Garden
3. Curvilinear Range
4. Succulent House
5. Aquatic Victoria House
6. Fern House
7. Alpine House
8. Orchid House
9. Great Palm House
10. Display House
11. Herbaceous Borders
12. Family Beds
13. Cherries
14. Annuals
15. Herb Garden
16. Chinese Shrubbery
17. Poisonous Plants
18. Rock Garden
19. Pond
20. River Tolka

ROWALLANE

COUNTY DOWN

The story of the gardens at Rowallane, County Down, famous today for their rhododendrons, starts with the sound of a sermon being preached on the back lawn. It is unlikely that the Rev. John Moore could have foreseen the future of the Pleasure Grounds of his modest farmhouse when he acquired the property in 1858. His improvements to the estate, including the planting of pines and other conifers, provided the much-needed shelter and height for the garden that was to be made by his nephew, Hugh Armytage Moore, who inherited the property in 1903. It is a relaxing garden to wander through, in part because the unpretentious layout of the original field pattern is still there, complete with ivy-covered walls and gates and soft springy turf. Informal paths lead through the different sections past stony outcrops of rock, down gentle declivities, and up gradual slopes. The planting flows harmoniously across and around the lie of the land, gently covering the slopes and encroaching onto the rocks.

Previous page, main picture: The stone pyramids of water-worn boulders were built by the Rev. John Moore and are one of the unusual features characteristic of Rowallane.

Previous page, detail: Wild maidenhair spleenworts cling to the stone walls.

Lining the avenue on the approach to the house are giant cairns that the Rev. John Moore built from piling up pyramids of huge round boulders, giving the first hint of the Victorian parson's craggy determination to leave his mark on the countryside that, when he arrived, was empty except for the furze and heather growing over the rocky fields. The avenue winds through the dark sumptuous plantings of conifers, beech, and immense rhododendrons, so you emerge into the light with the farmhouse, which is now the Regional Head Office of the National Trust in Northern Ireland, in front of you. Rev. Moore built the stables and the Walled Gardens, in which he mainly grew vegetables and fruit. However, apart from the specimen conifers, the Pleasure Grounds, and pond, he really concentrated on his oratory rather than his gardening, leaving the creation of the garden that we see today to his nephew.

Not only did Hugh Armytage Moore have good taste in the plants that he chose, but he also knew instinctively where to place them, making good use of the lie and fall of the land. The fact that County Down has such an important

group of gardens is perhaps no coincidence since it was also the home of a number of outstanding nurseries, such as Slieve Donard and Daisy Hill, now alas defunct. These certainly contributed to the plant material of the gardens, as well as being of benefit to both garden owners and nurserymen who were able to exchange seeds, plants, and knowledge. Also nearby, one of his sisters, Priscilla Cecilia, was planting what is now the National Arboretum. This fertile combination of circumstances, as well as the National Trust's continuing imaginative development, have all contributed to Rowallane's reputation as one of the most interesting gardens in the country.

Very little man-made landscaping has ever been carried out on the terrain, which coincides with William Robinson's theories of the importance of integrating garden plants into natural and seminatural countryside. The soil is acid and thin, overlying whinstone rock, and although at 40 inches the rainfall is low for Ireland, the air is always humid; the winter frosts are not severe, and the equable climate provides ideal growing conditions. Hugh Armytage

Moore was fortunate to inherit Rowallane at the beginning of one of the most exciting periods for gardening in Ireland and Britain. New plants were flooding in, especially from the Far East, collected by the intrepid plant-hunters, such as Ernest Wilson and Frank Kingdon Ward. He corresponded with them and subscribed to their expeditions, so he was able to raise many rare plants from their seeds, and these seedlings were planted all over the garden. With such a wealth of new material, "accidents" were bound to happen, and some of the accidental seedlings, hybrids of unrecorded parentage, turned out to be superb plants. To Rowallane's bees we owe the scarlet-blossomed quince *Chaenomeles* x *superba* 'Rowallane Seedling,' and the striking yellow St John's-wort *Hypericum* 'Rowallane Hybrid.' The candelabra primrose *Primula* 'Rowallane Rose,' was also a chance seedling. On the other hand, the Rowallane viburnum, *Viburnum plicatum* f. *tomentosum* 'Rowallane Seedling,' was probably just one of the countless seedlings raised from the collectors' lots. Moore planted an abundance of azaleas and the larger rhododendrons, including the fragrant, late-flowering *Rhododendron auriculatum* from central China, drifts of naturalized bulbs, and many rare and unusual trees. In 1942 the British Royal Horticultural Society awarded him the Victoria Medal of Honour for his work in his garden.

Starting at The Haggard, where in midsummer the cottony seeds of the Japanese poplar (*Populus maximowiczii*) cover the ground like snow, you walk through the gate to the Spring Ground. Here, in early Spring, old Irish cultivars of thin-petaled daffodils cover the grassy knolls. These are followed by the wildflowers among the grass, such as primroses, violets, butterfly

Opposite: A gate pier of jagged stone work beneath the tracery of branches the form the overhanging canopy of forest trees.

Opposite below: One of the small gates that still remain in the network of walls that divided the different fields in the original layout of the Rev. John Moore's pasture lands.

Below: Primula *'Rowallane Rose" was a chance seedling at Rowallane.*

orchids, spotted orchids, and horned poppies, and later by colonies of blue
devil's-bit scabious, as well as the unusual American blue-eyed grass
(*Sisyrinchium angustifolium*). Visitors flock to this area of the garden, perhaps
because it is a reminder of the days when drifts of color spread across hedge,
ditch, and field in spring all over the country.

At the end of the glade, there is a springtime explosion of color from the
massed banks of azaleas and rhododendrons, which are sheltered by pine,
beech, and oak. Specimen trees, such as Dawyck beech, stewartias, and a
bright-red-fruited crab apple (*Malus sargentii*), lead you to the famous Rock
Garden, where Hugh Armytage Moore dug out and displayed an outcrop of
stone, polished and scraped by glaciers thousands of years ago.
Rhododendrons are everywhere, and the beautiful *Primula* 'Rowallane Rose'
flourishes in groups of perennials by the streams.

In the Hospital there is a group of trees that are all native to the forests of
the Andes, but which are equally at home at Rowallane. The great southern
beech (*Nothofagus dombeyii*) towers above the huge bush of *Desfontainea
spinosa*, with its prickly hollylike leaves and yellow-mouthed scarlet tubular
flowers. A handsome *Cladrastris lutea*, the Kentucky yellow-wood with
wisterialike panicles of scented white blossom, stands next to the lady of the
woods (*Betula pendula*) and *Lomatia ferruginea*. A huge handkerchief tree
(*Davidia involucrata*) spreads its branches laden with the white bracts that
give it its English name, and ferns and foxgloves thrive beneath the canopy.

The L-shaped Outer Walled Garden is one of the most sheltered places in
the whole garden, with the sun beaming into it over the range of beech and
lime trees that shield it from the wind. The walls are made of bands of brick
and stone with porcelain tiles projecting through, enabling wires to be
threaded to tie up the plants. *Philadelphus* 'Burfordensis' leans over a seat
with the scent of *P.* 'Belle Etoile' drifting from around the corner. The South
American pineapple guava (*Feijoa sellowiana*), with crimson-and-white
flowers, fills one corner, and a euchrypia stands amid hydrangeas.

Holding aside a curtain of wisteria to walk through a gate, you come to
the Inner Walled Garden, where the National Collection of Penstemon is,
enclosed by hedges of boxwood clipped into cubes at each corner. In the
center of the next part of the garden, which is designed in the shape of a
Celtic cross, stands the original plant of Rowallane's own viburnum. A gate
lies ahead, leading onto crisply edged mown lawns, which beckon you towards
the Pleasure Grounds at the back of the house.

During World War II, the number of gardeners diminished and many of
the best-loved features became overgrown. The fact that the garden survived
this period is due to the care and attention of the Irish National Trust, which
acquired the property in 1954 and orchestrated a strong and imaginative
development program. It was also due to the work of Lady O'Neill of the
Maine who was instrumental in rescuing it, and after her to Graham Stuart
Thomas, and then John Sales, as well as to the head gardeners of the past and
to Mike Snowden, the head gardener of today.

Plan of Rowallane Gardens

1. The Haggard
2. Spring Ground
3. Rock Garden
4. Hospital
5. Outer Walled Garden
6. Inner Walled Garden
7. Pleasure Grounds
8. Pond

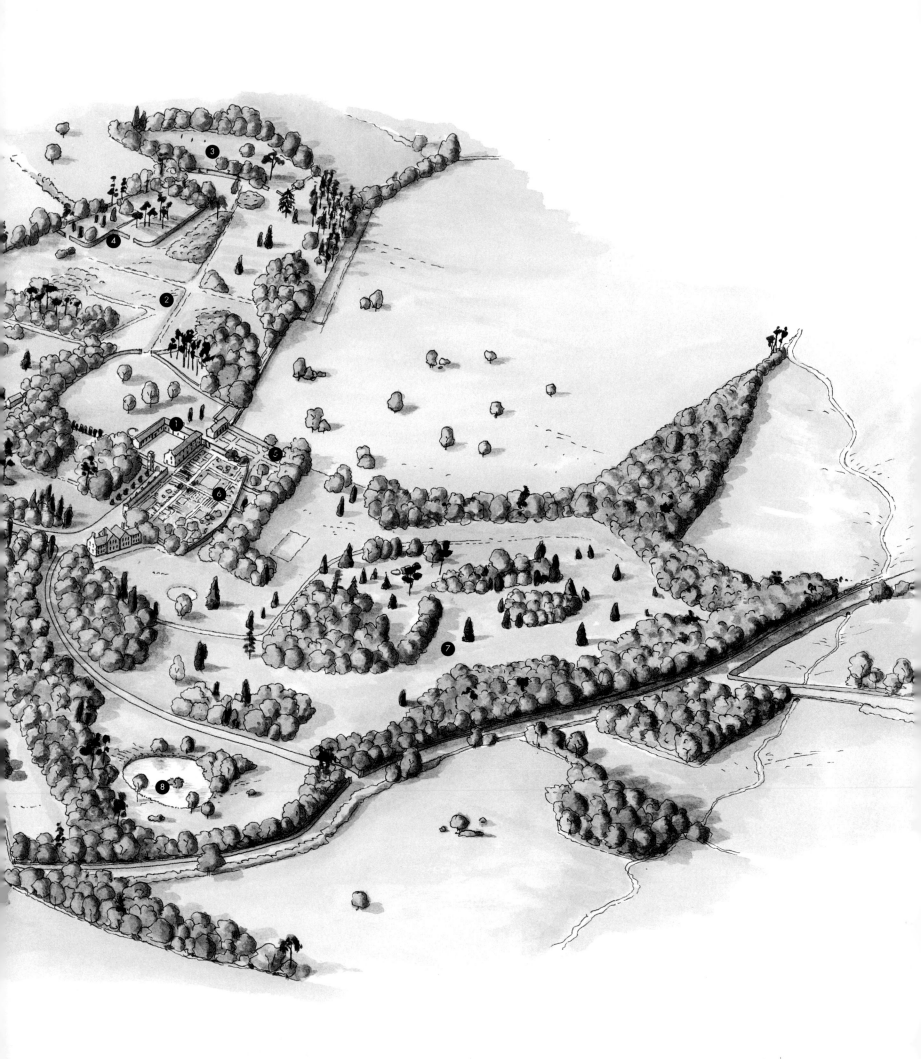

WOODFIELD
COUNTY OFFALY

Dr. Keith Lamb's private garden surrounding his eighteenth-century house at Woodfield, Clara, County Offaly, is a secret and magical place of many parts, vibrant with plant life. The house and garden which are located deep in the countryside near the Bog of Clara, have a settled, remote and mysterious quality.

An enchanting map of the demesne of Woodfield is illustrated with a watercolor showing the pedimented house as it was in 1765, with an embroidered formal garden enclosed in hedges with topiary, a hop yard, an orchard and rows of trees set in fields. The great bog is clearly marked. A fair-haired huntsman accompanied by his hounds chases a graceful fox across the top of the picture, while a stag dashes off to the right. The whole map is bordered by a ribbon of flowers including fritillaries, tulips, and roses – ancestors perhaps of some of the flowers that flourish at Woodfield today.

Previous page, main picture: In many Irish gardens, texture is as important as color. The rough gray limestone walls of the old farm buildings provide the perfect backdrop for the simple plain green fronds of a bank of ferns.

Previous page, detail: Blue-eyed Mary (Omphalodes Cappadocia) is just one of the many beautiful plants that thrive at Woodfield.

Twenty-five years ago, Dr. Keith Lamb joined the Kinsealy Horticultural Research Station as chief horticultural research officer. After a short time spent working on greenhouse crops, he started the Horticultural Nursery Stock Department, which dealt with the propagation and culture of trees and shrubs. Among his many achievements were his successful experiments proving that camellias would grow on moderately limy soil. With two colleagues, he wrote the *Nursery Stock Manual*, the basic handbook used by all nurserymen, adding to his reputation in the horticultural world. He wrote his thesis on the neglected subject of Irish apples, which involved endless traveling around the counties of Ireland, documenting the varieties of apples that he found in old orchards. He is a past president of the Royal Horticultural Society of Ireland and received their Medal of Honour in 1982 (which was a unique medal designed by Wendy Walsh and decorated with a fritillary). More recently, with Patrick Bowe, he has written *A History of Gardening in Ireland*, the only book available about the development of gardening in Ireland from prehistoric times to the present day. Despite all these accolades, Dr. Lamb possesses a modest diffidence of character, which is reflected in the intimacy of his garden at Woodfield. All the different elements around the house have been kept as they were, and he and his wife, Helen, have interleaved the garden very gently using the old trees as shelter.

When his older brother, Adam, died a bachelor, Dr. Lamb decided to retire early in order to live at Woodfield. He was delighted to find a totally overgrown Rockery, an ideal place to grow alpines – one of his great interests. The Lambs have traveled with the Alpine Garden Society to different mountain ranges and study the living conditions of the plants. In what had been the kennel yard behind the house, he built a series of eight raised beds, providing the well-drained soil that alpines enjoy in their native habitats. One of the unique features of Irish alpine gardening is the number of plants from the Southern Hemisphere that flourish here, and Dr. Lamb has had great success growing plants from Patagonia, New Zealand, and South Africa, alongside Irish natives and North American and Himalayan species.

In an area of under an acre, he has recreated in miniature all the sections you would expect to find in a much larger Irish garden. The old woodland avenue has been made into a garden. A wild garden has been developed inside the gray stone walls of the Old Bawn. Many plants were given by and exchanged with a spreading network of gardening friends, from Lord Talbot de Malahide of Malahide Castle, and Lady Moore at Rathfarnham in the old days, to Helen Dillon and Jim Reynolds today. The cheerful ghosts of old friends and their stories are attached to many of the plants that live on at Woodfield in their memory.

In early spring, the bare trunks and tangled branches of the ancient beech trees are underplanted with a brilliant carpet of bulbs. There are lots of different snowdrops, from the common wild snowdrop (*Galanthus nivalis*), both single and double, to the extraordinary 'Scharlockii,' which looks as if it has acquired a pair of donkey's ears. Dr. Lamb also grows the lovely Irish

snowdrop 'Straffan,' which arose at Straffan House in County Kildare when a snowdrop said to have been brought back from the Crimea by Major Eyre Massey after the Crimean War was crossed with the common one. The many daffodils include two dwarf ones, *Narcissus nanus* and *N. cyclamineus*, both from northern Spain and Portugal, which Dr. Lamb himself crosspollinated to produce 'Fairy Gold,' a very pretty, prolific and free-blooming golden-flowered miniature with a frilled trumpet. 'Fairy Gold' was named and officially registered only in 1998, although he had produced it in the early 1940s. Then there are the blue, white, double white, and yellow wood anemones, followed by spring-flowering cyclamen. Here are the speckled gray-green patterned leaves of *Cyclamen repandum*, with carmine flowers spotted and rimmed with red. Beneath the spreading branches of an old yew tree, the pink blossoms of *C. libanoticum* are quite at home even though far from their Lebanese home. Indeed, cyclamen from all around the Mediterranean nestle beneath the trees of Woodfield. *C. balearicum* from Majorca and nearby islands produces fragrant flowers each spring, while a Turkish species, *C. cilicium*, has slender pink-and-white blossoms in the fall. Also, in that season, the familiar *C. hederifolium* carpets the woodland garden, its delicate pink petals folded back like slim butterfly wings.

In spring and early summer, the woodland garden is awash with trinity flowers. The grandest one is the pure white *Trillium grandiflorum*, whose flowers often flush pink before the petals fall, and the most precious one is the rare double-flowered form of it. The California wake robin (*Trillium*

Opposite: Trilliums and dog tooth violets (Erythronium) *grow with great vigor at Woodfield, in the glades beneath the canopy of beech trees.*

Above: Early spring – trout lilies, daffodils, and hellebores are in bloom while the beech trees still have not sprouted new leaves.

chloropetalum), has red-and-white, pale pink, and dark red flowers, and is so content at Woodfield that it has seeded itself and is spreading over the limestone gravel of the drive. Dr. Lamb does not confine his trilliums to the woodland garden. In several of the stone troughs that are so typical of Irish country gardens, he grows the dwarf snow wake robin (*Trillium nivale*), which is just five inches tall and, though difficult to please, has seeded itself. There is also a pink species (*T. nivale*) form that originated in County Down.

At the top of the drive, near the house, is the original tree of a beautiful white-blossomed cherry that flowers very early in the year. This is 'Woodfield Cluster,' which Dr. Lamb raised himself in the 1940s. He had gathered fruit from a cherry tree growing in the grounds of the Albert College at Glasnevin, not far from the National Botanic Gardens, and this was one of the resulting seedlings. The weeping branches are thickly covered with deep rose-pink buds by the beginning of spring, and when they open the petals are pure white.

Turning left into the old walled garden you pass a pink rambling rose and to get into The Bawn – a verdant jungle. A mock orange (*Philadephus*) scents the air, and the ground is thick with primroses and foxgloves. This is a place where leaves count as much as flowers. The Chilean rhubarb throws gigantic green umbrellas over acanthus and pink-plumed rodgersias. The ivory trumpets of the Himalayan lily (*Cardiocrinum giganteum*) light up the green steamy shade; each spire is taller than the average gardener and bears about a dozen scented flowers. The spiky purple-leaved cabbage palm (*Cordyline australis*) presents a stark contrast, while the brilliant blue flowers of a *Corydalis flexuosa* catch the eye nearby. An *Arisaema* from the Himalayas, still labeled only with a collector's number, flourishes next to the white form of *Meconopsis*, whose flowers sway elegantly on slender stems. The climbing white rose that hangs over the empty stone window of the roofless stable came as a cutting from the last owner of Rosefields, where the Blackrock Clinic in Dublin now stands. In early spring, fresh green beech leaves provide the interest within the window frame, followed by the equally arresting tumbling summer roses and autumn sunsets. Ferns flourish both inside the stable and around the outside walls.

When I visited the Lambs, a great 12-foot high bugloss (*Echium pininana*) was flourishing by the front door of Woodfield, its bright blue flower spike lending an exotic touch to the simple lawn and the meadows beyond. But the bugloss, from the Canary Islands, dies after it has flowered, so it is unlikely to be seen again but seeds itself. Nearby, a *Cornus kousa*, whose white petals are tinged with pink, arrived as a seedling. Honeysuckle and wisteria climb the walls of the house, sheltered by beech trees and surrounded by a small bed. In the old fernery, there are hardy ferns of all sorts, including maidenhairs and hart's-tongues and one that looks like a very healthy clump of the curliest parsley. The fernery melds into the rockery, where every piece of ground is covered with contented plants, their pink, purple, white, violet, blue, and green starry faces glowing among the rocks. A stunning gentian – it has never been properly named – with flowers the color of lapis lazuli forms a perfect wreath. Dr. Lamb obtained this gentian many

Below: Not a single inch of space is wasted in this garden. Climbers cover the walls and even the nooks and crannies have been planted with succulent houseleeks.

years ago from the National Botanic Gardens at Glasnevin, and since it never sets seed, he has propagated it each year by taking cuttings. The sweetly scented pink-and-white-striped spathe of *Arisaema candidissum* is near *A. costatum* from China, looking as if it was made from stripy chocolate. The deep blue saucers of the mat-forming prostrate speedwell *Veronica prostrata* 'Trehane' carpet the rocks in front of the intensely yellow flower heads of the South African thistle *Berkheya macrocephela*.

In a sheltered nook against the house there are many other treasured plants, including colonies of the sumptuous blue poppy *Meconopsis x sheldonii*, hardy orchids such as the purple-flowered Kilmarnock orchid, which has densely spotted leaves, and the Russian foxglove. In a trough is a campanula, originally from Tully Nursery near Kildare when it belonged to Lord Wavertree. The head gardener was W.H. Paine, and the purple flowers splashed with white were named for him.

The airy perennial *Aquilegia formosa* with orange spires and yellow petals lines the peppermint-covered path, and a dark pink rose is tangled in syringa. A little sundial is ringed by a solid band of flowering geranium. An old yew shades the path edged by hellebores and ferns, and a strange plant whose leaves when bruised seem to smell of fox. The white baneberry (*Actaea alba*) flourishes in this shade and the black-and-white berries do indeed look like dolls' eyes, its other name.

All along the sunny south-facing wall of the old kennel yard hang different clematis, such as 'Rouge Cardinal,' with single crimson flowers, and 'Lasurstern,' with large blue ones. Hundreds of different plants are gathered here in the raised beds, including the insect-catching American pitcher plant

Below: In spring under the beech trees there is a multicolored carpet of magenta, cyclamen, blue-and-white wood anemones, and clumps of daffodils.

(*Sarracenia purpurea*) and its California cousin, the cobra lily (*Darlingtonia californica*). Although it is not a native Irish plant, the extraordinary pitcher plant is now found growing on a number of Irish bogs, including nearby Woodfield Bog, having been deliberately planted out over fifty years ago. At Woodfield the cobra lilies and pitcher plants share a peat-filled raised bed – a miniature bog – with heathers from Spain, cranberries, and the beautiful pink-flowered bog rosemary (*Andromeda polifolia*).

Dr. Charles Nelson, the taxonomist at the Botanic Gardens at Glasnevin for several decades, has written prolifically about many areas of gardening. In his book, *An Irish Flower Garden Replanted,* he drew attention to one of the most remarkable Irish ferns surviving from the Victorian era. It was found by a Mrs. Frizell in the mid-nineteenth century, growing between two large boulders on the Avonmore River at Castle Kevin in County Wicklow. It is known as the tatting fern because its fronds resemble the edging of pieces of lace, conjuring up a picture of a determined and conscientious Victorian lady with hat, trowel, and trug. In the shadiest part of the old kennel yard at Woodfield, there is a bed specially for miniature ferns, including Mrs. Frizell's elegant monstrosity.

The raised beds are in their prime in late spring and early summer. Little fritillaries and New Zealand mountain daisies (*Celmisia*) in variety mingle with dwarf irises, gentians, and phloxes. Over the side of one there is a cascading carpet of mountain avens (*Dryas octopetala*). This form is another Woodfield specialty and has recently been named 'Burren Nymph' because Dr. Lamb found it in the Burren where mountain avens grow in profusion. The flowers are double with many more than the expected eight petals, so they look like small white roses. 'Burren Nymph' came to Woodfield as a cutting and has proved its worth, so it is being multiplied by a local nursery for sale to gardeners everywhere. In another bed, Southern Hemisphere forget-me-nots with white and yellow, not blue, flowers flourish. Even the walls themselves are used – succulent houseleeks (*Sempervivum*) and fairy foxgloves (*Erinus alpinus*) grow in the cracks.

Standing at the back courtyard of the house with three lacy trees of *Robinia* x *hillieri* planted in the yard with their wisterialike panicles, with stone troughs full of plants, a white-walled slate-roofed barn, lilies in pots, lots more pots, a little greenhouse, and a glimpse of the rose through the empty stone window, one is struck by the feeling of activity and at the same time stability. It is obvious that this garden belongs to a man who has both peace of mind and clarity of thought. Although deaf from youth, Dr. Lamb misses nothing and can lip-read perfectly. He assures me that every single plant is in the best available position, and that each one gives its owner a lot of pleasure. As I am leaving, Dr. Lamb gestures to a low evergreen shrub bearing pink flowers positively bursting out of its trough. "*Philesia magellanica,*" he explains gently, and then with a wry smile and a twinkle in his eye, "usually regarded as rather difficult to grow...," which is probably as close to a boast as he'll ever get.

Above: Shuttlecock ferns are so called because of their resemblance to the feathered shuttlecock used in badminton. They are emerging from their winter covering in the roofless barn.

VISITOR'S GUIDE

ALTAMONT

Tullow, Co. Carlow

Phone +353 50 35 9444

Fax +353 50 35 9128

Times: April–October Sundays and Bank Holidays 2–6pm. Other days and times by request. Please check before visiting. **Facilities:** toilets; teas; craft shop; garden center with unusual plants; potager & herb garden; art gallery; wheelchair access. **Contact:** Colm McElwee

ANNES GROVE

Castletownroche, Co. Cork

Phone +353 22 26145 **Fax** +353 22 26145

Times: Mid-March–September Monday–Saturday 10am–5pm. Sunday 1–6pm. Other times by appointment. **Facilities:** toilets; buffet meals; guided tours by appointment; wheelchair access

Contact: Jane or Patrick Annesley

ARDCARRAIG

Bushy Park, Oranswell, Co. Galway

Phone +353 91524336

Times: Open strictly by appointment.

Facilities: Not suitable for wheelchairs or dogs; toilets **Contact:** Lorna MacMahon

Left to right: Altamont, Birr Castle, Butterstream, Glin Castle, Kilfane Glen and Waterfall, Mount Stewart.

BALLINLOUGH CASTLE GARDENS

Clonmellon, Co. Westmeath

Phone +353 46 33135 **Fax** +353 46 33331

Times: May–September. Tuesday –Saturday 11am–6pm. Sundays and Bank Holidays 2–6pm. Other times by arrangement. Closed first two weeks in August. **Facilities:** toilets; plants for sale; teas; guided tours by arrangement; limited wheelchair access. **Contact:** Sir John Nugent

BALLYMALOE COOKERY SCHOOL GARDENS

Shanagarry, Middleton, Co. Cork

Phone +353 21 646785

Fax +353 21 646909

Times: April–September 9.30am–6pm daily.

Facilities: toilets; guided tours; garden café and shop; limited wheelchair access.

Contact: Mrs. Darina Allen

BIRR CASTLE

Rosse Row, Birr, Co. Offaly

Phone +353 50 92 0336

Fax +353 50 9 21583

Times: 9am–6pm daily **Facilities:** toilets; guided tours; tea rooms; gift shop; plants for sale; wheelchair access. **Contact:** Brigid Roden

BUTTERSTREAM

Trim, Co. Meath

Phone +353 46 36017 **Fax** +353 46 31702

Times: April–September 11am–6pm daily.

Facilities: toilets; plants for sale; teas; wheelchair access. **Contact:** Jim Reynolds

CREAGH

Skibbereen, Co. Cork

Phone +353 28 22121 **Fax** +353 28 22121

Times: March–October 10am–6pm daily. Closed Tuesdays. Other times by appointment. **Facilities:** toilets; teas; wheelchair access; guided tours by arrangement. **Contact:** Martin Sherry

DERREEN

Lauragh, Killarney, Co.Kerry

Phone +353 64 83588 **Times:** April–September daily 11am–6pm. Other times by appointment. **Facilities:** toilets; teas; picnic area; guided tours for groups. **Contact:** Jacky Ward

THE DILLON GARDEN

45, Sandford Road, Ranelagh, Dublin 6

Phone +353 14971308 **Fax** +353 14971308

Times: March, July and August daily 2–6pm. April, June and September Sundays only 2–6pm. **Facilities:** toilets; plants for sale; guided tours by appointment. **Contact:** Helen Dillon

GLENVEAGH CASTLE

Glenveagh National Park, Co. Donegal

Phone +353 74 37088 **Fax** +353 74 37072

Times: Easter–October daily 10am–6.30pm. Mid-June–September, Sundays 10am–7.30pm. **Facilities:** toilets; teas. **Contact:** Ciaran O'Keeffe

GLIN CASTLE

Pleasure Ground & Walled Garden, Co. Limerick

Phone +353 68 34173 **Fax** +353 68 34364

Times: May–June, 10am–12 noon and 2–4pm daily. Closed Tuesdays. **Facilities:** toilets; parking; shop; guided tours of castle; limited wheelchair access; accommodation available.

Contact: Bob Duff

ILNACULLIN

Glengariff, Co. Cork

Times: March and October Monday–Saturday 10am–4.30pm. April, May, June and September Monday–Saturday 10am–6.30pm July and August Monday–Saturday 9.30am–6pm, Sundays 11am–7pm. **Facilities:** toilets; teas.

Contact: Finbarr O'Sullivan

KILFANE GLEN & WATERFALL

Thomastown, Co. Kilkenny

Phone +353 56 24588

Fax +353 56 27491

Times: April–September Sundays 2–6pm July and August daily 11am–6pm. Other times by appointment. **Facilities:** toilets; teas; car park; guided tours by arrangement

Contact: Mrs. Susan Mosse

KILLRUDDERY

Bray, Co. Wicklow

Phone +353 1 2862777

Fax +353 1 2862777

Times: Gardens: April–September 1–5pm daily. House: May, June and September 1–5pm daily. Groups on other dates and times by arangement.

Facilities: toilets; wheelchair access

Contact: Miss Ailbhe de Buitléar

MOUNT STEWART

Newtownards, Co. Down

Phone + 44 12477 88387

Fax + 44 12477 88569

Times: House and Temple of the Winds: Easter (April 2–11) daily 1–6pm April & October weekends 1–6pm May–September daily (except Tues) incl. Bank Holidays. Garden: March Sundays 2–5pm April–Sept daily 11am–6pm October weekends 11am–6pm **Facilities:** toilets; teas; wheelchair access

Contact: Harry Hutchman

MOUNT USHER

Ashford, Co. Wicklow

Phone +353 404 40116/40205

Fax +353 404 40205

Times: March 13th–November 2nd 10.30am–6pm daily. **Facilities:** toilets; teas; shops; parking; wheelchair access; guided tours can be booked in advance

Contact: John Anderson

NATIONAL BOTANIC GARDENS

Glasnevin, Dublin 9

Phone +353 1 8374388

Fax +353 1 83 60080

Times: Daily all year. Summer: 9am–6pm (Sundays 11am–6pm) Winter: 10am–4.30pm (Sundays 11am–4.30pm) **Facilities:** toilets; parking (limited); wheelchair access.

Contact: Donal Synnott

ROWALLANE

Saintfield, Co. Down, BT24 7LH

Phone + 44 1238 51031

Times: April–October, Monday–Friday 10.30am–6pm Saturday and Sunday

Facilities: toilets; teas; wheelchair access.

Contact: Mike Snowden

WOODFIELD

Clara, Co. Offaly

Phone +353 50 631161

Times: Open to garden clubs strictly by appointment. Not open to general public.

Facilities: Cars can park at the rear of the house but coaches stay at the road – 400m (500 yards) away. **Contact:** Dr. K. Lamb

INDEX

Page numbers in *italics* indicate illustrations.

A

Abelia triflora 201
Abies nobilis 25
Abutilon (mallow) 45, 63, 65 100, 120, 149
Acacia longifolia 100
Acer (maple) *45*, 48, 90, *190*
   walk at Mount Usher *187*, 193
Achillea ptarmica (sneezewort) *84*, 89
Acteae alba (baneberry) 218
Actinidia kolomikta 39
Agapanthus (African lily) 116, 197, 210
Agathis australis (Kauri pine) 151, 190
Alchemilla mollis (lady's mantle) 129
Allen family 61–7
Allium 49, 123, 87
alpines *117*, *119*, 120, 123, 214
Anderson, John 190
Andromeda polifolia 219
Anemone 28, *37*, *145*
Annesley family 33–9
Aquilegia formosa 218
arboreta 25, 35, 78
Arbutus unedo (strawberry tree) 168, 185
Arisaema 217, 218
Astilbe 47, 55
Aubretia 35, 78
Azalea 47, 48, 131, *186*, 209
Azara microphylla 'Variegata' 35, 99

B

bamboo 36, 77, 109, 110, 130
Beck, Leslie 65
beech *see Fagus sylvatica; see Nothofagus*
Begonia 'Red Devil' 178
Betula (birch) 28, 38, 47, 79, 209
Bigham, Mr and Mrs David 111
Billardiera longiflora 120
bluebells *34*, 54, *94*, 96, 108, 140
bog gardens 28, 47, 151, 219
Bomaria caldesii 119
boxwood 26, 29, 35, 67, *73*, 75, 78, 79, *84–5*
Brugmansia (angels' trumpet) 100, 149, *149*
Burkheya macrocephela 218
Bury, Viscountess 181

C

Callistemon (Australian bottle-brush) 45, 48, 67, 149
Camellia 85, 96, *105*, 140, 210
Campanula (bellflower) 63, *84*, 89, *89*
canals at Killruddery Gardens 16, *164–5*, 164–6
Cardiocrinum giganteum (giant lily) 179, 210, 216
catalpa 36, 210
Ceanothus (Californian lilac) 177, 193
Cedrus (cedar) 28, 39, 44, 139
Celmisia 'David Shackleton' 116
Cercidiphyllum japonica (katsura tree) 36, 131, *188–9*, 193

Chaenomeles x *superba* 'Rowallane Seedling' (quince) 208
Chamaecyparis 108, 110
Chilean fire bush *see Embothrium coccineum*
Cladrastis lutea (Kentucky yellow-wood) 209
Clematis 38–9, 47, *45*, 65, 120, 149
   C. 'Lasurstern' 29, 218
Clerodendrum trichotomum 25
Clethra alnifolia 11
Cordyline (cabbage-palm) 88, 140, 176, 180, 181, 217
Cornus 25, 36, 193, 210, 217
Corokia 149
cottage ornée at Kilfane 156, *156–7*, 158, 160
Crinodendron (lantern bush) 35, 67, 111, 139
Crocosmia 55, 88, *178*
Cryptomeria (Japanese cedar) 48, 110, *110–11*
Cupressus macrocarpa (Monterey cypress) 77
cycads *194*, 197
cyclamen 28, *33*, 39, 215

D

daffodils *45*, 77, 139, 209
Dahlia 88, *125*, *126–7*, 131
Darlingtonia californica (cobra lily) 219
Darmera peltata (umbrella plant) 36
Davidia involucrata (handkerchief tree) 28, 209
Delphinium 35, 63, 76, *84*, *115*
Desfontainea spinosa 209
Dicksonia antarctica 78, 99, 108, *108*, *109*, 111, 191
Dierama pulcherrimum (angels' fishing rods) 118
Digitalis (foxglove) 28, *54*, 87
Dillon, Helen 85, 115–23, 214
dogwood 35, 36, 47, 48, 140
Drimys winteri 111, 131, 139, 149
Dryas octopetala (mountain avens) 219
Dúchas, Department of Arts, Heritage, Gaeltacht and the Islands 11, 28, 128, 129, 196

E

Echium pininana (Canary Islands bugloss) 217
Embothrium coccineum 28, 35, 85, 96, 111, 151, 178
Emmenopterys henryi 201
Erica (heather) 55, 177
Erinus alpinus (fairy foxglove) 219
Escallonia 96, 130
Eucalyptus (gum tree) 48, 111, 180, 190
Eucryphia 25, 45, 47, 48, 130, 131, 167, 193
Euonymus bungeanus (Chinese spindle tree) 193
Eupatorium (hemp agrimony) 89

F

Fagus sylvatica (beech) *22*, *23*, 28, 38, 54, 65, *94*, 166
   F. 'Purpurea Pendula' (copper beech) 44
Feijoa sellowiana (pineapple guava) 210
ferns 47, 72, 78, 141, 156, 191, 198, 217, 219
Filipendula ulmaria (meadow-sweet) 36
Fitzgerald family 136–41
Fitzroya cupressoides (Patagonian cypress) 110
fruit gardens 54, 67
Fuchsia 39, 96, 141, *141*

G

Galanthus (snowdrop) 26, 45, 75, 140, 214, 215
Galega (goat's rue) 89

garden plans 30–1, 40–1, 50–1, 58–9, 68–9, 80–1, 92–3, 102–3, 112–3, 132–3, 142–3, 161, 172–3, 182–3, 192–3, 202–3, 210–11
garlic 38, 141, 191
gentian 217–8
Geranium wallichianum 'Buxton's Variety' 47
Ginkgo biloba 48, *163*, 167, 193
grapes 29, 140–1
Griselinia littoralis 'Bantry Bay' 148
Gunnera manicata 28, 36, 47, *77*, *77*, 96, 99, 138, 193

H

haha at Glin Castle 137
Halesia monticola (snowdrop tree) 193
handkerchief tree *see Davidia involucrata*
Harold-Barry family 95–6
hazel 43, 47, 48, 79
heather (*Erica*) 55, 177
Hebe (veronica) 179, 193
Hemerocallis (day lily) 48, 63, 76
Henry, Dr Augustine 21, 24, 72, 106, 116, 189, 201
herb gardens 29, 49, 62, *62–3*, 65–7
hermitage at Glin Castle *137*
Hoheria 36, 47, 131
holly 48, 65, 96
Holweia (lacebark) 193
honeysuckle *see Lonicera*
hornbeam *72*, 75, 90, 166
Hosta 28, 38, *44*, 54, 88, 179
Hydrangea 36, 47, 99, *153*, 178, 193, 210
Hypericum (St John's wort) 46, 208

I

Iris 36, 47, 76
Ixia caldesii 119
Italian gardens 130–1, 144–153, 179

J

Jay, Mrs Madeleine 187, 189, 191–3
Jekyll, Gertrude 21, 176, 179, 182
Juniperus recurva var. *coxii* 'Castlewellan' (coffin tree) 36, 190

K

Ker-Wilson, Charlotte ('Blot') 64
kitchen gardens 13, *29*, *60*, *61*, 67, *72*, 91, 99–100, 131, 140
Knautia macedonia (scabious) 89

L

Laburnum 35, 89
Lagarostrobus franklinii (Tasmanian Huon pine) 110, 149
Lamb, Dr Keith 213–19
Lamb, Peter 65
Lamb, Rachel 63
Lambert, Kenneth 101
Lansdowne, 5th Marquis 105–11
Lapageria rosea 176
laurels 28, 65, 99
Laurus nobilis (bay) 67, 140
Lavandula stoechas (French lavender) 53, 54, 55, *55*, 65
Leptospermum scoparium (tea tree) 149, 178
Leucojum (snowflake) 45